information
INSECURITY
PRIVACY UNDER SIEGE

BRENDAN JANUARY

TWENTY-FIRST CENTURY BOOKS / MINNEAPOLIS

Twenty-First Century Books
A division of Lerner Publishing Group, Inc.
241 First Avenue North
Minneapolis, MN 55401 USA

For reading levels and more information, look up this title at www.lernerbooks.com.

Main body text set in Adrianna 10/16. Typeface provided by Chank.

Library of Congress Cataloging-in-Publication Data

January, Brendan, 1972–
    Information insecurity / by Brendan January.
      pages cm
    Includes bibliographical references and index.
    ISBN 978-1-4677-2517-0 (lib. bdg. : alk. paper)
    ISBN 978-1-4677-8803-8 (eb pdf)
    1. Privacy, Right of—Juvenile literature. 2. Privacy—Juvenile literature. I. Title.
JC596.J36 2016
   323.44'8—dc23   2014018682

Manufactured in the United States of America
1 – PC – 7/15/15

CONTENTS

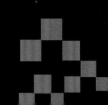

Many people don't realize that their digital data—everything from tweets to texts to images posted on Facebook—are saved in servers and might at some time be accessed by a school, a corporation, or a government agency.

INTRODUCTION

YOU ARE WHAT YOU TWEET

Imagine if someone followed you everywhere, opened your mail, read your diary, took secret photos of you, and listened to your conversations. This snooping would be considered a gross violation of privacy in the brick-and-mortar world, and in most cases, it would be illegal. But in the online world, such surveillance happens routinely, and it is not necessarily against the law. Social media, for example, allows your friends and even strangers to freely listen in on your conversations. Corporations and government agencies also routinely track your online activities, and much of this tracking is legal.

Many of the things we do every day—from communicating to learning to shopping and working—happen online. And all our online photos, posts, homework assignments, and purchases leave tracks, even if we delete them. Many organizations are following these digital tracks, gathering them together with tracks left by other users, and evaluating them to find trends and patterns. Many companies analyze these tracks to figure out how to sell more products. Government agencies, police departments, schools, insurance companies, and other organizations also look at this data. Digital systems "collect our photos, comments and friends in giant databases that are searchable and fair game for employers, university admissions personnel and town gossips," write Google chairperson Eric Schmidt and Google director of ideas Jarod Cohen. "We are what we tweet."

Schmidt and Cohen note that even deleted photos and posts remain stored in cyber databases, sometimes forever. And even if the stored information is untrue or no longer reflects a person's current feelings and opinions, it might still show up in an online search. As the years go by, "periods of people's lives will be frozen in time, and easily surfaced for all to see," the Google executives remark. "By the time a man is in his forties, he will have accumulated and stored a comprehensive online narrative, all facts and fictions, every misstep and triumph, spanning every phase of his life. Even the rumors will live forever."

THE PRIVACY TRADE-OFF

The Internet offers tremendous amounts of information, communication options, job opportunities, shopping, and entertainment—quickly, easily, and often at no cost. But in exchange for those benefits, many experts point out that we are losing something that was once taken for granted: privacy.

The right to privacy is the right to control whether or not your personal information is disclosed and to whom. Most nations recognize the right to privacy and have created laws and limits regarding the extent to which individuals, organizations, and government agencies can access private information.

But beyond the legal definitions and regulations, privacy is about something greater. It is about human freedom and the right to self-expression. As journalist Glenn Greenwald explains, "Ultimately the reason privacy is so vital is it's the realm in which we can do all the things that are valuable as human beings. It's the place that uniquely enables us to explore limits, to test boundaries, to engage in novel and creative ways of thinking and being. Only if we feel free of the kind of judgmental eyes of others are we able to try different things out, to experiment, to evolve, to free ourselves of mores [values] that are imposed on us or conventional orthodoxies [ways of viewing the world] about how we're supposed to behave and think."

The Internet makes it nearly impossible to avoid these "judgmental eyes of others." You might think that no one knows when you search online for help with a personal problem, something as private as drug addiction, depression, suicide prevention, or teen pregnancy. But in fact, that search will be stored in a database somewhere. And as long as it's there, someone will be able to access it. "We are brutally honest with search engines," elaborates computer security expert Mikko Hyppönen. "You show me your search history, and I'll find something incriminating or something embarrassing there in five minutes. . . . Search engines know more about you than your own family members. And this is all the kind of information we're giving away." A *New York Times* reporter described the situation this way, "You know that dream where you suddenly realize you're stark naked? You're living it whenever you open your browser."

In many cases, users sign away their privacy willingly. When users sign up for certain social media sites, apps, and streaming services, they must click on terms-of-service (or terms-of-use) agreements. These agreements often include privacy policies. They explain how much personal information the site will collect, how the data will be used, and to what extent it will be shared with outside groups. Most people automatically click to accept the agreements, but do not study them carefully. By accepting, users frequently give companies the right to follow their online activities and to share their data with third parties, such as advertisers and marketers. Many popular websites, such as Google, don't ask visitors to click on terms-of-use agreements, but policies listed deep in these sites explain that just by using them, visitors automatically give companies the right to analyze their data and to share it with outside groups.

SEARCH AND SEIZURE

Some of us don't mind trading privacy for the speedy searches, streaming entertainment, and extensive information available online. Some people aren't bothered by targeted online advertisements—tailored just for them, based on search and other online activities. But what many users don't know is that commercial businesses are not the only organizations tracking our online behavior. Government agencies are too. In the United States, police departments, state government offices, and federal organizations such as the National Security Agency (NSA) routinely gather data about US and non-US citizens, and much of this tracking is done in secret, without notification or terms-of-use agreements.

In the United States, laws such as the Privacy Act of 1974 and the Computer Matching and Privacy Protection Act of 1988 set forth rules about government gathering, handling, and sharing of personal data. In addition, the Fourth Amendment of the US Constitution protects citizens from unreasonable searches by the government. The amendment states that police and other government agents cannot search citizens' "persons, houses, papers, and effects" without a good reason and without authorization by a judge or a court. The amendment was enacted in 1791, long before the era of electronic communications. As technology evolved in the twentieth century, US courts expanded interpretation of the Fourth Amendment, ruling that it also protects citizens against electronic surveillance, such as the wiretapping of telephones by the police.

In the twenty-first century, as e-mail, texting, and wireless communication have become the norm, the courts are again looking at the Fourth Amendment and at other US privacy laws to update and refine limits on government searches. But US

When searching citizens' cars, homes, and possessions, the police and other government agencies must comply with guidelines set forth by privacy laws and the US Constitution. But the laws are less clear about limits on government snooping into our digital lives.

SECURITY ALERT

All vehicles entering a City of Phoenix parking facility may be subject to a search by the Phoenix Police Department. If you do not want your vehicle searched, please park at another facility located in downtown.

We are sorry for any inconvenience.

Please be patient.

ndard Parking   City of Phoenix

C.
B.

judicial and legal systems have not kept pace with the quickly changing world of technology. For this reason, Americans enter a legal gray area when they communicate in cyber space. In many cases, their most private digital communications might not be protected from government intrusion.

A DANGEROUS ROAD

Many US leaders argue that digital surveillance of citizens is critical to national security—especially in the fight against international terrorists. But such surveillance can also be dangerous. Throughout history, repressive governments have used information obtained via spying to intimidate, harass, arrest, and imprison citizens. For example, in the pre-Internet decades, in the former Soviet Union and the former East Germany, government security agencies used spies, secret cameras, and hidden tape recorders to monitor citizens' conversations and activities.

In the twenty-first century, repressive regimes have moved their spying online. For instance, the Chinese government carefully controls the Chinese Internet. The government blocks access to antigovernment websites and scans Internet traffic for searches or conversations about controversial or banned topics. The government also hires citizens to make pro-government posts on online chats and hires censors to flag and delete online antigovernment content. The Chinese authorities have shut down thousands of websites and businesses that have violated censorship rules. Similarly, in the Middle Eastern nation of Iran, a 250,000-person cyber police unit monitors all Internet activity, scanning blogs, chats, and websites for antigovernment or anti-Islamic views. (Islam is the national religion of Iran.) Anyone caught expressing such views online is subject to arrest.

Chinese and Iranian citizens are well aware that everything they post online is being monitored and that it might be used against them later—so they generally censor themselves online. Many scholars worry that digital monitoring in the United States could lead to similar self-censorship by Americans—and to the erosion of another right enshrined in the Constitution: freedom of speech. Award-winning journalist Nat Hentoff explains, "There are particular constitutional liberty rights that [Americans] have that distinguish them from all other people, and one of them is privacy." He says that losing privacy online "will have the effect of constricting freedom of expression. Americans will become careful about what they say that can be misunderstood or misinterpreted, and then too careful about what they say that can be understood. The inevitable end [outcome] of surveillance is self-censorship."

Many Americans fear that technology has put too much private information—and therefore too much power—into the hands of intelligence agencies, corporations, and other organizations. Many Americans fear that tracking will erode the democratic principles and freedoms on which the United States was founded. As technology writer James Gleick remarks about Google, a company whose slogan is Don't Be Evil, "We've all learned that the nicest people with the best intentions are capable of bringing evil into the world. No matter how sincere and idealistic [Google and other tech companies] are, they are concentrating an enormous amount of power in our informational universe in a very small number of hands."

In the United States and around the world, concerned citizens are sounding the alarm about digital privacy. Many have called for stricter controls on tracking by governments and corporations. A consensus on Internet privacy is not likely to emerge anytime soon. Meanwhile, unless you are willing to unplug completely, organizations and institutions of all kinds will continue to track your online activities. What rights do you have when it comes to privacy online? Who controls your digital data? How can you protect your personal data as you navigate the digital world? These questions are at the heart of the Internet privacy debate.

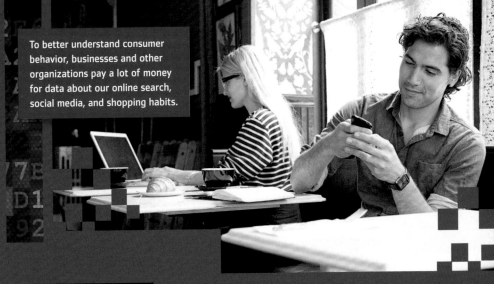

To better understand consumer behavior, businesses and other organizations pay a lot of money for data about our online search, social media, and shopping habits.

CHAPTER 1

PAYING WITH INFORMATION

Have you ever wondered why the social networking website Facebook is free? How does the company that offers so many free games, activities, and ways to communicate make money? Businesses that advertise on Facebook pay some of the company's bills. But the main way that Facebook and other free websites make money is by selling information about their users. "It's your data that makes Facebook worth $100 billion and Google worth $300 billion," explains journalist and *Mother Jones* magazine editor Monika Bauerlein. "You know how everything has seemed free . . . ?" adds *Time* magazine columnist Joel Stein. "It wasn't. It's just that no one told you that instead of using money, you were paying with your personal information."

Data is valuable. Advertisers want to know which customers are interested in which products. Medical insurance companies want to know who is healthy and who is sick. Politicians want to know whether people are more likely to vote for a specific candidate or political party. Banks want to know which

people are most likely to pay back their loans on time. Police departments want to know if one suspect has talked to another suspect via cell phone. National governments want to know which individuals belong to terrorist cells.

In earlier eras, before the Internet, it wasn't easy to collect such data. Researchers and marketers had to comb through telephone books, driver's license records, birth and death records, voter registration lists, and other public information to compile data on individuals. This process was inefficient and time-consuming. The Internet changed data collection completely. In the twenty-first century, companies gather data instantaneously by tracking people via their computers and smartphones.

In her book *Dragnet Nation: A Quest for Privacy, Security, and Freedom in a World of Relentless Surveillance*, award-winning investigative journalist Julia Angwin outlines the major types of digital trackers. Government trackers include agencies such as the Internal Revenue Service (the US tax collection agency) that gather data on people in the normal course of doing business; law enforcement agencies such as local police departments and the Federal Bureau of Investigation (FBI); and intelligence agencies such as the National Security Agency. Commercial trackers include retail businesses that collect data on their customers to learn more about who is purchasing what; search and social media companies such as Facebook, Twitter, and Google, which provide free services while also gathering data on users; marketers and advertising agencies, which use digital data to place targeted ads on people's computers; and data brokers that buy data from government and commercial sources, analyze it, and resell it to businesses, political groups, government agencies, and other organizations.

> **"Personal data is the new oil of the Internet and the new currency of the digital world."**
>
> —Meglena Kuneva, former commissioner for consumer protection of the European Commission, 2009

FORTUNE COOKIES

In many cases, tracking begins when a user visits a website to shop, search for information, or communicate on social media. The site automatically, with or without a user's permission, installs a file called a cookie onto the visitor's web browser. The cookie assigns the browser a number. When the visitor returns to the website using the same browser, the site recognizes the assigned number and remembers the user's log-in information, preferences, and past activities on the site. In addition to cookies, companies might place additional tracking tools on visitors' browsers. One tool, called a beacon, can track cursor movements on a web page and capture words that people type into websites, such as messages in comment sections.

In addition, most websites allow third parties, such as advertisers, marketers, and data companies, to install cookies, beacons, and other tracking files on the browsers of those who visit the site. Third parties not only track users' activities on individual sites but also track users from site to site across the web. By visiting just a single website, you can unknowingly install hundreds of third-party tracking files onto your browser. Julia Angwin wrote in the *Wall Street Journal (WSJ)* that when she used a test computer to visit Dictionary.com, a site that offers free dictionary and thesaurus services, 234 third-party organizations put tracking software on the computer's browser. "When I go to TIME.com as a user, I think only TIME.com is collecting my data," adds Nicole Wong, deputy general counsel at Google. "What I don't realize is that for every ad on that page, a company is also dropping a code [tracking file] and collecting my data. . . . Sometimes you're not even sure who the advertisers are." Many web browsers allow users to disable or reject cookies from certain websites, but "some [tracking] tools surreptitiously re-spawn themselves even after users try to delete them," says Angwin.

By monitoring the sites that people visit and what users do on those sites, advertisers, marketers, and data brokers are able to build profiles of web users. Angwin gives the example of Ashley Hayes-Beaty. In 2010 a data company called Lotame Solutions put a thirty-two-character alphanumeric code on Hayes-Beaty's web browser. By following this code around the web, Lotame Solutions learned that Hayes-Beaty was a twenty-six-year-old woman from Nashville, Tennessee. It learned that her favorite movies were *The Princess Bride*, *50 First Dates*, and *10 Things I Hate about You* and that she liked the TV show *Sex and the City*.

This data isn't very personal—it's the type of information people might willingly post on Facebook. But Lotame Solutions didn't get this data from Facebook—it simply tracked Hayes-Beaty through her browser. And trackers are capable of ferreting out much more private data, such as financial and medical information. By amassing more and more data over time, trackers can develop a very accurate profile of an individual. And profiles such as these are extremely valuable to retailers and other organizations that want to pinpoint new customers.

SMARTER THAN YOU

Smartphones gather even more information than cookies on web browsers. This is partly because a smartphone can serve as many devices at once—a cell phone, MP3 player,

Telephones companies, tech companies, and other businesses can track your cell phone wherever it goes. In this way, the businesses also know where you are.

camera, radio, audio recorder, video recorder, and web browser. Smartphones serve so many functions, writes tech expert Fred Vogelstein, that they "have become extensions of our brains."

And our brains are being watched. Most smartphone users enthusiastically download apps and breeze through and accept terms-of-service agreements. But by agreeing to the terms of service, users are giving data companies the right to constantly monitor their online activities and even their global positioning system (GPS) locations. In this way, aggregators know precisely where someone is when he or she is using a specific app. Many apps collect this information without even asking a user to agree to terms of service.

A 2011 *WSJ* investigative report revealed that many of the most popular mobile phone apps routinely send user information to third-party companies. Of the 101 apps tested by the *WSJ*, "56 transmitted the phone's unique device identifier to other companies without users' awareness or consent. Forty-seven apps transmitted the phone's location in some way. Five sent a user's age, gender and other personal details to outsiders. At the time they were tested, 45 apps didn't provide privacy policies on their websites or inside the apps."

Another *WSJ* article noted that users generally have no way to opt out of such tracking. It's "nearly impossible to prevent cellphone 'apps'—games and other software—from transmitting information about a phone and its owner," the article stated. Smartphone companies have tried to address privacy concerns by outfitting phones with systems that tell users when and how they are being tracked and that give them options for disabling tracking. But critics say these systems are often confusing, misleading, and ineffective.

WHO'S WHO?

Data companies claim that the information they gather and sell usually identifies people only by numbers, not by name. But privacy advocates say that the concept of nameless profiles is laughable. They note that it's not hard to attach a name to a trove of other data, especially if you know someone's age, gender, income, and other personal information. Finance blogger Aaron Pressman relates that "even data [stripped of] personal references can be reconnected to individuals." He notes one case in which researchers from the United States and Belgium studied a bundle of user profiles provided by a cell phone carrier. All the names and other personal data had been removed, but by analyzing GPS time and location data from the profiles, the researchers were able to correctly name 95 percent of the users. In another study, researchers at Carnegie Mellon University in Pittsburgh, Pennsylvania, found a way to uncover people's Social Security numbers by looking at only birthday and hometown information provided on social networking sites.

Constitutional Amendments at the Heart of the Internet Privacy Debate

The First Amendment

"Congress shall make no law respecting an establishment of religion, or prohibiting the free exercise thereof; or abridging the freedom of speech, or of the press; or the right of the people peaceably to assemble, and to petition the government for a redress of grievances."

The Fourth Amendment

"The right of the people to be secure in their persons, houses, papers, and effects, against unreasonable searches and seizures, shall not be violated, and no warrants shall issue, but upon probable cause, supported by oath or affirmation, and particularly describing the place to be searched, and the persons or things to be seized."

How much do data companies know about you? One company, Acxiom, says it wants to demystify data collection and make it less threatening for computer users. Acxiom is a leader in the data-gathering industry. It collects details on seven hundred million consumers and sells those details to more than seven thousand client companies. In 2013 it launched a website called AboutTheData.com. The home page states, "Know what data says about you and how it is used." Acxiom chief executive officer (CEO) Scott Howe explained, "We are trying to be incredibly transparent . . . you can't build trust if you are holding stuff back."

One writer tested the site in the summer of 2014. He logged in using his name, address, birthday, and e-mail address. The website then revealed data that Acxiom had collected on him. The profile correctly identified his gender, race, and education level. It said that he was married, liked music, and had a white-collar job. It stated that he had children but incorrectly identified the number (three instead of two) and got their ages wrong. It listed the value of his house and his household income. It revealed that he and his wife had used a credit card to buy clothing, home furnishings, gardening products, and software. Except for misidentifying his children, the data was accurate.

AboutTheData.com allows users to correct errors in their Acxiom profiles and to opt out of receiving advertisements based on the company's data. They cannot delete their profiles altogether, however.

Acxiom, based in Little Rock, Arkansas, is one of the largest data businesses in the world. It collects information about what people view, post, and purchase online, analyzes the data, and sells it to groups that want to precisely target customers.

Privacy advocates have criticized the site. They say it shows just a small sample of the vast amount of personal data the company actually collects and that it merely serves to put a good front on Acxiom's operations. "This is an industry [data collection] that largely works in the shadows," remarked Chris Soghoian of the American Civil Liberties Union (ACLU). "Unless you know every company and every company provides an opt out, there is no way to protect your data from these firms."

If you shop online for skate shoes, you'll probably see more adds for skate shoes on your browser in the following days. That's because your browsing activity is being tracked. Advertisers buy information from tracking companies to learn more about other products you're interested in.

CHAPTER 2

IT'S ABOUT PROFIT

Have you ever noticed that after you search online for a pair of shoes, that same pair of shoes—and similar pairs—often shows up in advertisements on other websites you visit? Here's how it works: Suppose you look at shoes on the Zappos website. A type of business known as a data exchange has placed a tracking code on the Zappos site. When the tracker recognizes that you are interested in a certain style of shoes, the data exchange instantly sells your browser ID information to other businesses that want to reach shoe buyers. The purchasers then advertise shoes on additional web pages that you visit.

Targeting individual shoppers is one way to advertise online. Another is to target groups of consumers based on their data profiles. Remember Ashley Hayes-Beaty, who lived in Nashville and liked watching romantic comedies? Once Lotame Solutions had determined that Hayes-Beaty enjoyed romantic movies, it could package her profile with the profiles of thousands of similarly minded moviegoers (identified only by numbers, not by names) and sell the profiles to companies that wanted to pitch their products to people who liked romantic movies. Or Lotame Solutions could sell a batch of profiles to companies that wanted to advertise to southern women in their twenties.

Facebook bundles and sells its data the same way. In his book *The Facebook Effect*, technology journalist and author David Kirkpatrick describes an early example of such bundling. In 2005 a record company wanted to promote Gwen Stefani's "Hollaback Girl," a pop single whose video includes cheerleaders doing chants and routines. To find buyers who might be interested, the record company could have hired an advertising agency that placed cookies on web browsers, followed users around the web, and built profiles of their interests. With this data, the agency could then have tried to identify pop music enthusiasts, particularly young women who were interested in cheerleading. This technique can be imprecise, however. A cookie can't tell exactly who is using a web browser. A friend or a younger sibling might jump on someone's computer and visit sites that the main user normally wouldn't, blurring that person's data profile. With those drawbacks in mind, the record company decided to take a different approach. It contacted a new website called Thefacebook, which at the time had about 5.5 million college student users. Thefacebook sorted through its database of users and produced a list of people who had either expressed an interest in cheerleading or identified themselves as cheerleaders. It sold this list to the record company, which targeted those individuals with ads on their web browsers. The record company knew that its advertising would reach those most likely to embrace it and mostly likely to buy Stefani's single. Kirkpatrick says that "'Hollaback Girl' did become a popular cheerleading anthem at [college] football games that fall. It's impossible to prove the ads on Thefacebook were determinative, but it's a fair bet that just about every cheerleader at the schools where Thefacebook operated saw them."

Of course, Thefacebook became Facebook, and by 2014, the site had nearly 1.25 billion users. It had become a leader in scientific marketing—that is, marketing based on statistical analysis of data. As the website Marketing-Schools.org explains, "Facebook gathers data about user age, location, preferences, and even topics used in personal posts or conversations. This data is then analyzed and used to plan marketing strategies, from the targeted advertisements that appear on the side of your Facebook profile, to websites that Facebook thinks you will 'Like.'"

THE MONSTER UNDER THE BED

In 2011 *Time* magazine columnist Joel Stein e-mailed a friend in Houston, Texas, saying that he might come to visit. Stein soon noticed an ad for a Houston restaurant above his Gmail in-box. Had someone been reading Stein's e-mail? No. Instead, a tracking file on his browser had scanned his e-mail and identified him as a Houston-bound individual. His browser ID number had then been bundled with the ID numbers of hundreds of other Houston-bound people and sold to an advertiser. That business placed Houston-specific ads on those individuals' browsers.

Stein noted that this kind of data collection is bothersome because it "seems so creepy," but data businesses defend the process, saying that it does a good job of matching consumers with products in which they are really interested. "We no longer want to receive mass marketing—getting bombarded with ads that have no relevancy to our lives—because it's intrusive and wastes our time," explains the AboutTheData.com home page. Hooman Radfar of the web tracking company AddThis puts it more bluntly. Data analysis allows users to see "ads that don't suck," he says.

Advertisers say that targeted ads are much more effective than nontargeted ads. That is, they are more likely to entice customers to buy. And data companies always stress that people whose data is bought and sold are not identified by name. "It's the monster-under-the-bed syndrome," Russell Glass, CEO of a data mining company, told *Time* magazine. "People are afraid of what they really don't understand. They don't understand that companies like us have no idea who they are. And we really don't [care]. I just want a little information that will help me sell . . . an ad."

ON TARGET

How do analysts use data to increase sales? Many companies closely guard their strategies. They don't want to let competitors know their secrets, and they don't want to unnerve customers by revealing how much personal data they are collecting. But a *New York Times* reporter was able to interview Andrew Pole, a data strategist working for the Target Corporation, a large retail chain. Pole gave the reporter a fascinating and detailed picture of how a corporation tries to get an edge on its competition by digging for very personal information about its customers.

Specifically, Target wanted to know which customers were pregnant. To Target, pregnant customers (and their partners) are sales opportunities. Target stocks a broad range of goods in its stores, but customers typically come to Target to buy only specific items. When a couple has a baby, however, their old routines are turned upside down. They no longer have the time or energy to visit many different stores. They are often exhausted and are looking for one-stop shopping.

Privacy Slips through the Cracks

In addition to the Fourth Amendment of the US Constitution, various federal and state laws protect the privacy of citizens' personal information, such as medical, educational, banking, and driving records. For instance, the federal Health Insurance Portability and Accountability Act (HIPAA), passed in 1996, guards the privacy of medical records and spells out to what extent health insurers, health-care providers, pharmacies, and other businesses can use or disclose that information without a patient's permission.

But as with many other privacy regulations, the Internet has allowed groups to sidestep HIPAA without breaking the law. For example, HIPAA prohibits the sale of individuals' health data for marketing purposes, but if names are removed from the data, it can be sold. Julia Angwin reports in *Dragnet Nation* that many pharmacies make big money by collecting such data and selling it to national pharmaceutical databases. Technically, no one's privacy is being violated, but as studies have shown, it's not at all difficult to link names with unidentified data, in this case potentially exposing patients' private medical histories to prying eyes.

Target marketers knew that if they could figure out which customers were going to have babies, the company could then advertise to them that virtually everything they might need—from diapers and baby bottles to food, electronics, and home goods—could be found at Target stores. For a harried parent with a newborn, that would be a welcome message. It would also help Target increase sales.

Many retailers know when women have babies because birth records are public documents. As a result, parents are usually bombarded with dozens of advertisements after a baby is born. Target wanted to get its message to parents *before* they had a baby, and the company's researchers believed that the second trimester of pregnancy (from the third to the sixth month) was optimal. "We knew that if we could identify them in their second trimester, there's a good chance we could capture them for years," said Pole, who masterminded the program to look for pregnant customers. "As soon as we get them buying diapers from us, they're going to start buying everything else too."

Pole began by looking at all the data Target had compiled on its customers. Like other big retailers, Target tracks customer purchases. When someone shops at a Target store with a debit or credit card, Target assigns the cardholder a guest ID number. Customers who buy online also get guest ID numbers. The company tracks ID numbers to build profiles of shoppers and their purchases over time. Another source of data is Target's baby-shower registry, where pregnant women sign up for Target products that they'd like to receive as gifts. The *New York Times* reported that by gathering its own data and buying additional data from third parties, Target creates detailed profiles of customers, including

> your age, whether you are married and have kids, which part of town you live in, how long it takes you to drive to the store, your estimated salary, whether you've moved recently, what credit cards you carry in your wallet and what Web sites you visit . . . your ethnicity, job history, the magazines you read, if you've ever declared bankruptcy or got divorced, the year you bought (or lost) your house, where you went to college, what kinds of topics you talk about online, whether you prefer certain brands of coffee, paper towels, cereal or applesauce, your political leanings, reading habits, charitable giving and the number of cars you own.

Using this data, Pole could figure out when certain customers had been pregnant (since Target had data on their children and when they were born) and what they had purchased during pregnancy. His analysis of the data revealed that pregnant women often bought unscented skin lotion at the beginning of their second trimester. Before getting halfway into their pregnancies, many women bought bottles of calcium, magnesium, and zinc dietary supplements. With these and about twenty-five other clues about female shoppers who might be pregnant, Pole created a "pregnancy prediction program." He used it to sift through the profiles of tens of thousands of female Target shoppers.

Once Target had identified women who might be pregnant, it could send them ads and coupons for cribs, baby clothes, and other baby products. But Target didn't want shoppers to know that it was studying their shopping habits and possibly learning about their intimate, private lives. This might have unsettled many customers and led to a public relations disaster, the company knew. So when it communicated with possibly pregnant customers, Target mixed baby-related offers in among random ads that had no relation to babies. Company marketers knew that three baby-specific ads might look suspicious, but a baby ad next to an ad for lawnmowers and wineglasses would probably not raise eyebrows. Target's strategy worked. The *New York Times* reported that "soon after the new ad campaign began, Target's Mom and Baby [department] sales exploded."

Target got some pushback for invading shopper privacy. In one case, a seventeen-year-old girl began receiving baby-related coupons from Target. Her father was so angry that he stormed into his local Target store and asked to see the manager. He

Businesses gather and purchase data about customers' finances, interests, and shopping habits. Target Corporation used such data to determine which customers were soon to have babies and then sent them coupons for baby-related items.

demanded to know why his high-school–age daughter was receiving coupons on baby items. "Are you trying to encourage her to get pregnant?" he asked.

As it turned out, Target was aware of something the girl's father didn't know. His teenage daughter was pregnant. Target hadn't broken any laws in sending coupons to the girl, "but even if you're following the law, you can do things where people get queasy," Pole admitted.

Critics take a harsher stance. They say that data-gathering tactics such as Target's would be illegal in the offline world. "If I tell my best friend I'm pregnant over the phone or by letter . . . it's a crime for someone to listen in or to open the letter," writes Chicago-Kent College of Law professor Lori B. Andrews. "Yet if I provide the same information in an email or through Skype, data aggregators can collect and sell the information without my consent."

WEBLINING

Data analysis is often used for a simple purpose—to advertise more effectively so as to sell more products and earn more money. This can seem innocent, but companies have been known to use online profiles to discriminate against certain customers. Redlining—or discriminating against specific racial, ethnic, or other groups when doing business—is against the law. But experts say that weblining—a cyber version of redlining—routinely takes place online, with no repercussions for groups that discriminate.

"The tech industry has little interest in protecting your or my privacy. Indeed, it is precisely the opposite. Leading tech companies have a clear economic motive for intruding upon our privacy and obtaining as much data and personal information as they can. It's about profit, and it allows them to serve you up more targeted advertising."

—James Steyer, founder of Common Sense Media,
a safe technology advocacy group, 2012

Banks have begun to use weblining to weed out borrowers they feel are not creditworthy and are not likely to pay back loans. In one case, the marketing company Media6Degrees analyzed social media patterns and noted that borrowers who paid back loans on time tended to be online friends with other borrowers who paid back loans on time. Those who were late in paying or who defaulted (didn't pay at all) tended to be friends with others who were late or who defaulted. Using this information, Media6Degrees compiled lists of potentially creditworthy and non-creditworthy individuals and sold them to banks. Banks often examine loan applicants' past financial data to determine whether they might be creditworthy. But in this case, people were put into categories based simply on their online friendships.

Similarly, one man was deemed less creditworthy based on the behavior of other shoppers. He returned from his honeymoon and discovered that his American Express credit limit (the total amount he could charge on his American Express credit card) had been lowered to $3,800 from $10,800. The company told him the limit had been reduced because "other customers who have used their card at establishments where you recently shopped have a poor repayment history with American Express."

"Stereotyping is alive and well in data aggregation," wrote Lori B. Andrews in the *New York Times* in 2012. "Your application for credit could be declined not on the basis of your own finances or credit history, but on the basis of aggregate data—what other people whose likes and dislikes are similar to yours have done. If guitar players or divorcing couples are more likely to renege [default] on their credit-card bills, then the fact that you've looked at guitar ads or sent an e-mail to a divorce lawyer might cause a data aggregator to classify you as less credit-worthy."

Andrews also notes how weblining could be used to reinforce class and gender stereotypes. "When young people in poor neighborhoods are bombarded with advertisements for [vocational] schools, will they be more likely than others their age to forgo college?" asks Andrews. "And when women are shown articles about celebrities rather than stock market trends, will they be less likely to develop financial savvy?

Advertisers are drawing new redlines, limiting people to the roles society expects them to play."

Digital business expert Michael Schrage, in the *Harvard Business Review*, says that large amounts of data give businesses invaluable insights. He also stresses that such insight can also result in discrimination. He illustrates his point with an exaggerated example, describing how a company might learn the following information:

> Single Asian, Hispanic, and African-American women with urban post [ZIP] codes are most likely to complain about product and service quality to the company. Asian and Hispanic complainers happy with resolution/refund tend to be in the top quintile [fifth] of profitability. African-American women do not. Suburban Caucasian mothers are most likely to use social media to share their complaints, followed closely by Asian and Hispanic mothers. But if resolved early, they'll promote the firm's responsiveness online. Gay urban males receiving special discounts and promotions are the most effective at driving traffic to your sites.

It's easy to see how discrimination could result from such racial- and gender-based profiling. Suppose a real estate company didn't want to rent or sell apartments to people of a certain race. With data mining, the company could filter those people from its targeted advertising, instead directing sales pitches only to members of racial groups with which it desired to do business.

Profiles like those compiled by Acxiom and other aggregators usually include people's race and gender. Such information is available in public records and is simple for data aggregators to obtain. But even with supposedly anonymous data, it's not hard to figure out someone's race, gender, or sexual orientation. To prove this fact, researchers at Cambridge University in Great Britain looked at the Facebook "Likes" of fifty-eight thousand users and were able to predict (with up to 95 percent accuracy) whether each person was a man or a woman, white or black, and gay or straight. "Data is not color blind, it's not gender blind," emphasizes Microsoft researcher Kate Crawford.

CHAPTER 3

AN OPEN BOOK

In early 2014, an American couple—Robert Barefield and Stephen Mazujian—were vacationing in the Southeast Asian nation of Cambodia. After climbing to the top of the Angkor Wat temple, Mazujian suddenly collapsed and died. A few months later, Barefield made a Google search to look for tributes to his partner. Among the search results, he was horrified to see a gruesome picture of Mazujian's body from the hospital morgue in Cambodia.

Barefield believes the photo was taken by a police officer, who had either given or sold the picture to a Cambodian website. Barefield asked Google to remove the photo from the company's search results, but Google refused. Google told him to ask the Cambodian website to remove it. Barefield tried but made no headway. Google executives were sympathetic but unyielding. They said that as long as the posted image did not violate copyright laws (laws that give creators the exclusive right to publish, sell, distribute, and reproduce their work), it would remain in Google's search results.

BAD DECISIONS

The story of the photo from the morgue is not unusual. Once images make their way to the web, they remain there, possibly forever. In 2010 a thirteen-year-old Washington State girl named Margarite learned that the hard way. She snapped a cell phone photo of herself, nude, in her bathroom mirror and texted it to her new boyfriend. After the couple broke up, he forwarded the photo to one of Margarite's old girlfriends. The second girl typed beneath the photo, "Ho Alert! If you think this girl is a whore, then text this to all your friends." She sent the photo to everyone on her list of contacts.

By late the next day, the former boyfriend had been handcuffed by police and taken to a county juvenile detention center. The girl who forwarded the photo was taken to juvenile detention as well, along with another girl who had helped spread the photograph. They were charged with dissemination of child pornography, which is a felony under US law. If convicted, the students could have been placed in a juvenile detention center for up to thirty-six weeks and been registered as sex offenders. After a deal with the prosecutor, the three teens were sentenced to perform community service instead. They were directed to create educational material for other young adults about the actions that had gotten them in trouble.

Although the ordeal was stressful for everyone, Margarite's father pointed out that his daughter was particularly harshly impacted and for the long term. She will never be free of the experience, since the nude photo—like everything posted to the Internet—can eventually be found, even if it's deleted from individual phones or computers. At the end of a mediation session with the teens and their families, Margarite's father said, "When you walk out of here tonight, it's over, you're done with it. Keep in mind that the only person this will have a lasting impact on [is my daughter]. She will have to live with this for the rest of her life."

The father's words were soon proved right. When a friend tried to cheer up Margarite by taking her skating, she was recognized at the rink from the nude picture. The friend was jeered on his Myspace page for hanging out with Margarite. Hoping to avoid further attention, Margarite transferred to another school, but she soon learned that her picture had arrived there first. Whispers and taunts surrounded her. Margarite returned to her old school, where she still had some friends and figured she had nothing to hide. When a reporter asked what she would tell someone who was about to text a similar picture, she replied, "Don't do it at all. I mean, what are you thinking? It's freaking stupid!"

Some Hollywood stars have learned the same lesson about keeping private photos offline. In the summer of 2014, unknown hackers broke into the iCloud accounts of a number of Hollywood actors, stole nude photos of the celebrities, and posted them online. *Hunger Games* star Jennifer Lawrence, one of the victims, was infuriated. "It is not a scandal. It is a sex crime," she said. "It is a sexual violation. It's disgusting."

A Hollywood entertainment lawyer, representing more than a dozen of the victims, threatened a $100 million lawsuit against Google, which was slow to remove the photos from its search results and from various Google-owned sites, such as YouTube. "Google knows the images are hacked stolen property, private and confidential photos and videos unlawfully obtained and posted by pervert predators who are violating the victims' privacy rights," wrote the attorney. "Yet Google has taken little or no action to stop these outrageous violations." The lawyer further argued that many of the photos were selfies—created by the actors themselves and therefore protected by US copyright law. By law Google must remove search results that link to copyrighted material. The threat of a lawsuit pushed Google to remove links to the images, but they are still available in cyber space to those with enough determination and technical know-how to find them.

Hoping to avoid similar embarrassment, millions of users signed up for the online messaging service Snapchat, which launched in 2011. The

Hackers stole nude photos of Jennifer Lawrence and other celebrities by breaking into their iCloud accounts. People around the world are realizing that nothing stored on a digital device can be kept private with certainty.

service allows users to send videos and photos that disappear a few seconds after viewing. The images are not stored on servers, which makes Snapchat a popular app for those concerned about Internet privacy. About 50 percent of Snapchat users are between the ages of thirteen and seventeen. Some users, including many teens, have used the service for sexting—or sending naked or sexually suggestive pictures of themselves—secure in the idea that the pictures would disappear and not be stored online. That security was shaken in October 2014 with the news that unidentified hackers had broken into a third-party app frequently used with Snapchat. By some reports, the hackers had stolen two hundred thousand Snapchat pictures and videos taken over several years and posted them on the website 4chan.

What the Hack?

The Internet privacy debate has centered on government surveillance and corporate tracking. But another group routinely intrudes on online privacy. Criminal hackers work relentlessly to break into cell phones and computers to steal passwords, bank account numbers, credit card numbers, corporate secrets, military secrets, and more. As witnessed by the iCloud and Snapchat hacks of 2014, hackers also steal photos that people would prefer to keep private.

Users can protect their phones and computers by installing Internet security software, but the software is not foolproof. In the United States, major banks, retailers, and even the US military have been hacked. More and more, computer users have lost faith that their personal data will be kept private. "I'm not sending super scandalous stuff over Snapchat anyway because it does not seem secure," said college freshman Sarah Bounab after the Snapchat hack. She continued, "I feel like anything can get leaked these days, or hacked into."

Technology writer Sarah Perez noted that some commentators blamed the victims after both the iCloud and the Snapchat hacks. "Some of those watching the fallout from the recent hacks shamed the victims for their actions. *Tsk, tsk, tsk. Shouldn't have taken those naughty pictures in the first place!*" But Perez goes on to stress, "People do and say things that aren't always logical or well thought through. You have, too. Everyone has recorded something on their phone—text, video, photos—that they wouldn't want exposed to the world. Some things are private. Not even because they're X-rated or illegal. Just because they're private."

SCREEN TEST

Many teens regularly post pictures of themselves at parties. Some pictures show underage drinking, illegal drug use, and other risky behavior. But the web is an open book, and digital evidence of such misbehavior can have serious consequences for young adults. Many teens don't realize that college admissions officers routinely turn to the web to screen applicants. A 2011 survey revealed that almost one in four admissions officers at 359 selective colleges consulted Facebook when reviewing applicants. One in five admissions officers used Google.

Employers also use the web to check out job seekers. In a 2010 survey, three out of four job recruiters and human resource managers said that they researched job candidates online. They looked at social networks, photo- and video-sharing sites, personal websites, and blogs. Another 70 percent reported that they had ruled out job candidates due to what they had found online. Twenty-two-year-old Connor Riley was one of those candidates. After she received a job offer from the computer networking company Cisco Systems, she tweeted, "Cisco just offered me a job! Now I have to weigh the utility of a fatty paycheck against the daily commute to San Jose [in California] and hating the work." After that, Cisco withdrew the job offer. "We here at Cisco are versed in the web" was the company's response to Riley's tweet.

University of Texas freshman Maxwell Birnbaum made a more serious mistake in 2012. He was riding in a van with friends when a police officer pulled them over and searched their bags. The officer discovered six ecstasy pills in Birnbaum's knapsack. He was arrested and taken to a police station, where officers took his mug shot. Birnbaum was not sent to jail, but for several years, he had to attend counseling, take drug tests, and visit with a judge. The record of his arrest was expunged, or wiped off the books.

All the same, a number of websites acquire mug shots from police departments and post them online. Such publication is legal, since mug shots are a matter of public record. If the charges against someone have been dropped or the arrest record has been wiped clean, the sites will remove the mug shot, but the person has to pay several hundred dollars for this service.

With his drug arrest behind him, Birnbaum applied for an internship with an elected state representative, and like many employers, the representative's office did a Google search on Birnbaum's name. The top four search results linked to his mug shot. "The assistant to this state rep called back and said, 'We'd like to hire him, but we Google every potential employee, and the first thing that came up when we searched for Maxwell was a mug shot for a drug arrest,'" recalled Birnbaum. "I know what I did was wrong, and I understand the punishment, but these Web sites are punishing me, and because I don't have the money it would take to get my photo off them all, there is nothing I can do about it." In late 2013, after national reporting on mug shot sites and cases such as Birnbaum's, Google changed its search equations, so that most mug shots no longer show up at the top of search results. But unless someone pays for removal, the photos are still available on mugshots.com and similar sites.

IN YOUR FACE

Facebook has been criticized for failing to keep its users' information private. It's true that Facebook lets users control their own privacy settings—to determine how much of their personal information will be revealed publicly and how much will be revealed only to friends on the site. But critics say the privacy settings can be hard to understand and that the company has pushed users to reveal more rather than less information about themselves.

In 2009, for instance, Facebook changed its privacy procedures without warning users and without asking them to approve the changes. The new procedures made public many items that users had designated as being private. And even after some users deleted their accounts, Facebook left their photos and videos on the site for others to see. "Facebook is nudging the settings toward the 'disclose everything' position," said Marc Rotenberg, executive director of the US Electronic Privacy Information Center. "That's not fair from the privacy perspective."

Users were unsettled again when Facebook introduced its Timeline feature in 2010. Previously, users could bury their old posts, photos, and videos under new updates, making the older material hard to find. With Timeline, users can browse a person's entire Facebook history relatively quickly. "This may be the first moment that many of Facebook's 800 million members realize just how many digital bread crumbs they have been leaving on the site—and on the Web in general," wrote a *New York Times* reporter. "For better or worse, the new format is likely to bring back a lot of old memories. But it could also make it harder to shed past identities—something people growing up with Facebook might struggle with as they move from high school to college and from there to the working world."

In some cases, Facebook's attitude about privacy has had painful consequences. In one instance, a young woman named Bobbi Duncan, a lesbian college student, wanted to keep her sexual orientation a secret from her family. In 2010, when she joined the Queer Chorus, a gay choir at the University of Texas, the president of the group added her name to the choir's Facebook discussion group. Unbeknownst to Duncan, Facebook then automatically informed all her Facebook friends—including her father—that she had joined the choir.

Page Turner

How much data does Facebook have on you? In 2010 an Austrian law student named Max Schrems looked for an answer to that question. He requested all the data Facebook had collected about him in the three years since he had joined the site. Under laws of the European Union (EU, a political and economic organization of twenty-eight European nations), Facebook was required to comply with the request. (US law does not require Facebook to comply with similar requests from Americans.)

Max Schrems poses with a 1,222-page document listing all the information Facebook had collected on him over the course of three years.

Facebook sent Schrems a 496-megabyte pdf that ran 1,222 pages. The company had sorted information about Schrems's Facebook activity into fifty-seven categories, including a list of computers he had used to log on to his account. The document included every message, chat, contact, and post he had ever made on Facebook, including material that he had deleted.

Facebook had outed Duncan to her family. Her father was particularly hostile when he learned of her sexual orientation. The situation threw Duncan into despair, and she tried to commit suicide. "I blame Facebook," she said. "It shouldn't be somebody else's choice what people see of me."

The Federal Trade Commission, a national agency charged with protecting consumers and preventing unfair business practices, investigated Facebook and concluded in November 2011 that the company had engaged in unfair and deceptive practices when it changed its privacy procedures in 2009. The company agreed to undergo user privacy assessments, carried out by independent firms, every two years for the next two decades. In 2015 it added a "Privacy Basics" feature, an interactive guide that helps users understand and personalize their privacy settings.

Police monitoring of video surveillance is increasingly common in cities across the United States and Europe.

CHAPTER 4

SURVEILLANCE STATE

On November 10, 2009, an assistant principal at Harriton High School in Rosemont, Pennsylvania, called student Blake Robbins into her office and handed him a photo. It showed Blake in his bedroom holding small colored objects. The assistant principal said the objects looked like pills, perhaps illegal pills. The school charged Blake with dealing drugs and contacted his parents.

The question of Blake's innocence was quickly cleared up. The objects in the photo were not drugs but pieces of Mike and Ike candy, Blake explained. But another question remained: how did school administrators get a picture of Blake in the privacy of his own room?

The situation began in 2008 when the Lower Merion School District, which includes Harriton High School, decided to issue free laptop computers to its teachers and students. "Every high school student will have their own personal laptop," said the district's superintendent, "enabling an authentic mobile 21st century learning environment."

Unbeknownst to the students, however, the school district had signed up for a service called TheftTrack. The system was supposed to be activated if a computer was reported stolen or missing. Once activated, TheftTrack would take a screenshot and a photograph with the computer's built-in camera every fifteen minutes, as well as when the computer was turned on or off or came out of sleep mode. In theory, the images would help lead school administrators to the missing laptops.

But the school district didn't use the system this way. In several cases, when computers were reported missing, school district staff turned on TheftTrack as planned. But after the laptops had been located and returned to students, district staff didn't turn off the tracking system. As a result, TheftTrack continued to take photos and screenshots for weeks afterward. In additional cases, for unknown reasons, staff members activated the tracking system on computers that were not missing. In total, TheftTrack took more than thirty thousand photos and more than twenty-seven thousand screenshots from student laptops and sent them to the school district.

One boy's computer took about one thousand images—469 from the webcam and 543 screenshots—and sent them to the school district. "When I saw these pictures, it really freaked me out," said the boy. Another student who was photographed said that she had had her laptop open while she was "getting changed, doing my homework, taking a shower, everything."

After the situation became public, the FBI, the nation's top law enforcement agency, investigated the case to determine whether the school district had broken federal wiretapping laws. The FBI eventually dropped the case because it could not establish beyond a reasonable doubt that the school district had intended to break the law when it instituted the laptop program.

Meanwhile, the Robbinses and another student's family filed civil (noncriminal) lawsuits against the school district. The families sought compensation for invasion of the students' privacy and also demanded that the district halt its surveillance of students and teachers. A judge complied with the request, ordering the school district to discontinue its collection of images and to destroy the ones it had gathered. (All students and their families were permitted to see the images first.) As part of the settlement, the district paid $610,000 to compensate Blake and the other student and to pay their families' legal fees.

CAMERA READY

Although it is illegal to secretly photograph people in the privacy of their own homes, it is not illegal to photograph them in public places. For many years, banks, convenience stores, and other businesses have used video cameras to monitor customers near and inside their establishments. In the event of a theft

or other crime at the store, law enforcement can review the video footage to try to identify suspects. Some believe that video cameras can also deter crime. The idea, although unproven, is that when people know they are being filmed, they are less likely to break the law.

In big cities such as New York, the police use security cameras and license-plate readers to monitor activity on public streets. The images can help police officers identify criminal suspects.

Many cities have also set up surveillance cameras to deter and fight crime and to search for suspected terrorists. New York's Lower Manhattan Security Initiative is a network of four thousand video and license-plate-reading cameras set up in public places in the southern part of the city. New York Police Department officers monitor feeds from the cameras, along with feeds from cameras installed by private businesses in and around their property, twenty-four hours a day. In Great Britain, the city of London set up its surveillance program in 1998. Called the Ring of Steel, the system uses nearly five hundred thousand cameras, as well as license-plate readers and other devices, to monitor public spaces in central London.

In the United States, such public surveillance has helped solve certain crimes. For example, in April 2013, two bombs exploded near the finish line at the Boston Marathon, killing three spectators and injuring more than 260 spectators and runners. To find the bombers, Boston police sifted through video footage from police cameras and private security cameras and pictures taken by bystanders with cell phones. Three days later, the FBI released pictures of two suspects, whose images had been captured by cameras mounted outside a department store. The two men, Chechen brothers from the Caucasus region of Russia, were quickly identified. One died after a shootout with police. The other went into hiding but was arrested a day later.

Video surveillance is even more effective when combined with facial recognition software, which scans photos of faces and maps facial features. The software measures the distance between a person's eyes, the shape of the nose, the length of the forehead, and other facial dimensions. It can also detect a person's gender, approximate age, skin color, and even mood. All that information can then be stored in a database.

In 2013 a department store surveillance camera captured this image of the Boston Marathon bombers, helping police identify and apprehend them.

Police are increasingly using facial recognition software to identify those photographed by surveillance cameras. Officers scan the images and then search for matches in huge databases of previously stored photos. In September 2014, the FBI launched its Next Generation Identification system. The system includes a database of more than fifty million photographs, including mug shots, photos taken for employee background checks, and images from security cameras. Police departments across the nation can tap into the system, which also includes a database of fingerprints. By 2015 the system is expected to handle more than fifty-five thousand photo searches per day.

BIG BROTHER IS WATCHING

Surveillance cameras and facial recognition programs promise to help law enforcement identify suspects, but privacy advocates worry that the government might also use them to spy on citizens. "We like to think we have some privacy in our lives, that we can go places that we don't necessarily want the government to know about," said Jennifer Lynch of the Electronic Frontier Foundation. "What concerns me is if all those cameras get linked together at some point, and if we apply facial recognition on the back end, we'll be able to track people wherever they go." The *New York Times* editorial board agrees. In 2013 the board wrote, "Using facial-recognition software to match databases of photos with images from security cameras in public spaces and private buildings can help law enforcement agencies spot and track dangerous criminals. But the same technology can just as easily be abused to target political activists or protesters."

Such targeting is commonplace in many repressive nations. For instance, not only does Iran employ a 250,000-member cyber police force to look for antigovernment and un-Islamic online activity, in January 2012, the Iranian government directed all Internet cafés to install security cameras. The businesses must also keep records of customers' online activity at the cafés.

"Surveillance changes history. . . . People will change their behavior online because they know anything they say online can be used against them in the future."

—Mikko Hyppönen, computer security expert, 2014

Such repression is not supposed to happen in the United States. Americans are free to worship as they desire, to assemble peacefully, to express themselves freely, and to protest against the government—all rights protected by the First Amendment. But civil libertarians charge that government agencies have begun to violate these rights, often with the help of digital technology. For instance, after foreign Islamic terrorists attacked the United States with hijacked airliners on September 11, 2001 (9/11), the New York City Police Department launched widespread surveillance of Islamic Americans in New York and surrounding states, simply because they practiced the same religion as the hijackers. According to the ACLU, this surveillance program included undercover spies pretending to be Islamic, photo and video surveillance of mosques (Islamic houses of worship), and a vast intelligence database containing details about the lives of thousands of Islamic Americans.

The explosion of smartphone technology in the second decade of the twenty-first century has made such surveillance even easier. For example, before the presidential elections in 2012, protesters gathered outside the Republican National Convention in Tampa, Florida, to express opposition to policies supported by the Republican Party. During the protests, undercover police officers walked through the crowd, secretly taking cell phone photos and videos of individual demonstrators. The effort was intended to make sure that the protests remained peaceful and to identify anyone who behaved violently or unlawfully. But privacy experts worry that such surveillance could have a chilling effect—discouraging citizens from speaking out against the government for fear of being singled out by facial recognition software and then arrested. "We shouldn't just accept that undercover police will infiltrate peaceful protesters exercising their First Amendment rights, photograph them, and use face recognition or other techniques to identity them. We must not come to accept the existence of a secret police in our society," wrote Jay Stanley, a policy analyst with the ACLU, after the convention.

Civil liberties groups worry also about secret cell phone tracking by law enforcement. National Public Radio reported in 2014 that many police departments use devices called IMSI (international mobile subscriber identity) catchers. These machines send out signals like those used by cell phone towers. Normally, when portable devices receive the signals, they report their identifying information and location to the cell towers—that's how users get widespread

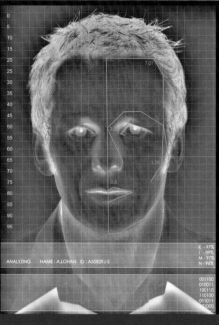

With facial measurements, the police can more precisely identify individuals in photos. Privacy advocates warn that facial recognition systems could lead to excessive monitoring of citizens' whereabouts and activities.

cell phone service as they travel around a city or a larger area. IMSI catchers send out the same signals, only stronger, and essentially trick cell phones into sending ID and location information to the police. Capturing such data can help police and other authorities track down criminals who have cell phones. But civil liberties groups note that this data collection is often done without search warrants, that nonsuspects are also being tracked, and that police departments are very secretive about IMSI use.

The FBI also tracks suspects electronically. According to a 2006 ABC News report, in some cases, FBI agents have taken remote control of suspects' cell phones, using the phones' microphones as secret listening devices. A 2013 *Washington Post* story revealed that the FBI also uses sophisticated surveillance software to covertly retrieve files, photographs, and e-mails from suspects' computers and to remotely turn on computer cameras to take secret photographs and videos of suspects in their homes and offices. Agents access suspects' computers and phones the same way that criminal hackers do: they send out phishing e-mails, tricking suspects into clicking on links that load spyware onto their machines. The article reported that the FBI requests search warrants before carrying out such spying. In one case, a judge denied such a request, ruling that the spying violated the suspect's Fourth Amendment rights. But even with search warrants, the practice alarms civil libertarians. "We have transitioned into a world where law enforcement is hacking into people's computers, and we have never had public debate [about the practice]," said the ACLU's Christopher Soghoian.

AN EVEN BIGGER BROTHER IS WATCHING

In August 2012, an eight-minute video appeared on the *New York Times* website. The filmmaker was Laura Poitras, who had previously produced documentaries about the Iraq War (2003–2011) and the US War on Terror (2001–present). The *Times* video featured William Binney, who had worked for thirty-two years as a code breaker, data analyst, and mathematician at the NSA.

The NSA is one of the nation's top intelligence organizations. Since its founding in 1952, the agency has sought out information about foreign threats to the United States, including terrorist threats. But Binney reported that after the 9/11 attacks, the NSA began using its spying tools to target not just foreigners but also US citizens. He described an operation called Stellar

Wind, which carried out warrantless surveillance to compile profiles of US citizens, in violation of the Fourth Amendment. "This is something the KGB, the Stasi, or the Gestapo would have loved to have had about their populations," said Binney, referring to the secret intelligence agencies in the Soviet Union, East Germany, and Germany under the Nazi Party in the 1930s and the mid-1940s. Binney had resigned his position at the NSA to protest the program.

In January 2013, about six months after the video first aired, Poitras received an anonymous e-mail that asked for her public encryption key, so that the e-mailer could send messages that only she could read. Poitras provided the key, and the stranger began to send encrypted, or coded, messages, promising to provide proof of secret government surveillance programs.

Poitras was in the process of producing a longer documentary about US government surveillance. She was suspicious that these messages were some kind of setup—designed to get her and those she was interviewing for the film in trouble with the government. But the messages kept coming and the sender kept promising, "This I can prove."

The writer also suggested that Poitras work with Glenn Greenwald, who would be able to publicize the information he wanted to disclose through a major news outlet. Greenwald, a lawyer and journalist, had written extensively about the loss of US civil liberties after 9/11. Poitras reached out to Greenwald, who read the e-mails and "felt intuitively that this was real."

The anonymous e-mailer was Edward Snowden. He had worked for the NSA as a technology contractor. In this job, he had helped manage the NSA's computer systems, which gave him access to virtually all the agency's digital files. Using a relatively simple program called a spider, Snowden had sifted through and copied about 1.7 million NSA documents. These documents revealed extensive details about global NSA spying operations, much of it carried out without warrants.

In May 2013, Poitras and Greenwald met with Snowden outside a restaurant in Hong Kong. Snowden took the two journalists to his hotel room. Once inside, they took the batteries out of their cell phones and placed the phones in the room's refrigerator. The refrigerator walls provided a barrier against radio waves in the event that someone was trying to take remote control of the phones. The trio propped pillows along the hotel room door to muffle any sound that might leak into the hallway.

Poitras set up a camera, and Greenwald began to ask Snowden questions about NSA spying on US citizens. The interviews continued over the next several days. In addition to these interviews, Snowden provided a series of NSA documents to Poitras, Greenwald, and another reporter, Barton Gellman. The information he revealed included the following:

- The NSA had used a secret court order to monitor phone records of millions of US customers. The court order had required phone companies to turn over to the NSA customer billing information and call records.
- Tech companies such as Yahoo, Google, Facebook, Microsoft, and Apple had complied with NSA orders to turn over user information—all in secrecy and without warrants.
- The NSA had, without the companies' knowledge, hacked into private data traffic between Yahoo and Google.
- The NSA had collected more than 250 million address books from Americans' Yahoo, Hotmail, Gmail, and other e-mail accounts in a single year.

- The NSA had cracked widely used encryption codes designed to keep private information secure.
- The NSA had been gathering location data on five billion cell phones per day.
- The NSA had listened in on phone calls and read the private e-mails of world leaders, including leaders of nations that were friendly with the United States.

With documents leaked by Snowden, Greenwald reported on NSA spying in the *Guardian*, an award-winning British newspaper. Gellman published additional pieces in the *Washington Post*. The revelations began a global conversation about privacy and national security.

A poll by the nonpartisan Washington, DC–based Pew Research Center and the *Washington Post*, taken in June 2013, shortly after the first revelations, showed that 56 percent of Americans felt it was acceptable for the government to collect phone data to fight terrorism; 41 percent felt the data collection was unacceptable. The survey also revealed that 62 percent of Americans thought it was important for the government to investigate terrorist threats, even if the process intruded on personal privacy, whereas 34 percent said that the government should not intrude on privacy, even if this hampered the investigation of terrorist threats. As for the government monitoring of e-mail, 45 percent of respondents said that this was acceptable in the effort to prevent terrorist attacks; 52 percent said it was unacceptable. (These numbers don't total 100 percent per question; the remaining respondents answered "don't know" to the questions.)

While the American public was almost evenly divided about spying and privacy issues, many commentators and scholars were outraged by the revelations. Many compared the NSA to intelligence agencies in totalitarian regimes, just as William Binney had done. "The NSA now has an interception machine that East Germany's Stasi could only have dreamt about," wrote filmmaker Oliver Stone and historian Peter Kuznick. The *New York Times* editorial board also condemned the NSA, charging that the surveillance came at the expense of Americans' fundamental rights. NSA monitoring of phone records "fundamentally alters the relationship between individuals and their government," wrote the editorial board. "The effect is to undermine constitutional principles of personal privacy and freedom from constant government monitoring. . . . The government's capacity to build extensive, secret digital dossiers on such a mass scale is totally at odds with the vision and intention of the nation's framers [founders]."

World leaders who had been spied upon also expressed outrage. Brazilian president Dilma Rousseff, one of the NSA's targets, announced at the United Nations, "In the absence of the right to privacy, there can be no true freedom of expression and opinion, and therefore no effective democracy." Rousseff canceled a 2013 visit with US leaders to protest the spying, and in the fall of 2013, many Brazilians sarcastically added lines in their e-mails wishing the NSA a good day or a Happy Thanksgiving.

Many groups took action to protect themselves and their citizens from the snooping eyes of the US government. Some foreign organizations moved their data from US cloud-storage servers to servers in Europe, where privacy laws are stronger. Big tech companies around the world added extra layers of encryption to protect their customers' data. And tech experts began talking about the potential for "splinternets," exclusive national Internet systems that would be walled off from the Internet in other nations. Experts and scholars also expressed concern that the NSA infringement on privacy would lead to self-censorship and limits on free speech.

DEFENDING THE NSA

The NSA defended one of its data gathering programs, called PRISM, launched in 2007 under President George W. Bush to fight terrorism. NSA leaders explained that the agency needed a vast amount of data to find what they referred to as a "needle in the haystack." In this case, the haystack was the data and the needle was any terrorist who might write a text, make a phone call, or send an e-mail. The NSA said that it had to sift through massive numbers of messages to find patterns and communication networks that would help uncover potential threats to national security.

General Keith Alexander, former director of the NSA, called the PRISM program a valuable yet controversial "hornet's nest" that "enables the NSA to see threats from [terrorist bases in] Pakistan and Afghanistan and around the world." He continued, "My concern is that, without knowing the facts, people will say, 'Let's put that hornet's nest away.' *We* [the NSA] sure would like to get rid of that hornet's nest. We would like to give it to somebody else, anybody else. But we recognize that if we do that, our nation now is at greater risk for a terrorist attack."

While defending the NSA, many US leaders denounced Snowden, saying that he had undermined the nation's security by leaking top-secret documents. "He's a traitor," said John Boehner, Speaker of the House of Representatives. "The disclosure of this information puts Americans at risk. It shows our adversaries what our capabilities are. And it's a

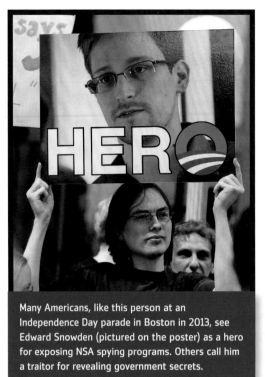

Many Americans, like this person at an Independence Day parade in Boston in 2013, see Edward Snowden (pictured on the poster) as a hero for exposing NSA spying programs. Others call him a traitor for revealing government secrets.

giant violation of the law." President Barack Obama added, "If any individual who objects to government policy can take it into their own hands to publicly disclose classified [secret] information, then we will not be able to keep our people safe, or conduct foreign policy. Moreover, the sensational way in which these disclosures have come out has often shed more heat than light, while revealing methods to our adversaries that could impact our operations in ways that we might not fully understand for years to come."

Edward Snowden faces charges of espionage and other crimes in the United States and is currently in exile in Russia, from where he continues to speak out against government surveillance. Laura Poitras has taken refuge in Berlin, Germany, to protect herself from ongoing US government surveillance and harassment. "There is a filter constantly between the places where I feel I have privacy and don't," she said, "and that line is becoming increasingly narrow. I'm not stopping what I'm doing, but I have left the country. I literally didn't feel like I could protect my material in the United States."

Although some viewed him as a traitor, many Americans saw Snowden as a hero for blowing the whistle on the NSA.

And for their reporting on Snowden and the NSA, in 2014 the *Washington Post* and the *Guardian* won one of the highest journalism honors in the United States—the Pulitzer Prize for Public Service. The Pulitzer organization stated that the newspapers' "aggressive reporting" had sparked "a debate about the relationship between the government and the public over issues of security and privacy."

REPERCUSSIONS

In late 2013, a special commission appointed by President Obama published a report on the NSA's surveillance programs and processes. In the report, titled *Liberty and Security in a Changing World*, the commission made forty-six recommendations, many of them designed to restore confidence in the agency and the federal government after Snowden's revelations. For example, the commission recommended that the NSA end its practice of collecting and storing phone records. The commission suggested that, instead, such data should be maintained by phone companies or other parties and turned over to the NSA only by court order.

Around the same time, two US citizens filed a lawsuit against the NSA, charging that the agency's collection of phone data was illegal and that any records of their calls should be destroyed. The judge hearing the case agreed. "I cannot imagine a more 'indiscriminate' and 'arbitrary invasion' than this systematic and high tech collection and retention of personal data on virtually every single citizen for purposes of querying and analyzing it without prior judicial approval," said Richard J. Leon, a US District Court judge. "Surely, such a program infringes on 'that degree of privacy' that the founders enshrined in the Fourth Amendment."

The New *1984*

In handing down his ruling on the NSA phone surveillance program in December 2013, Judge Richard J. Leon described the agency's gathering of data as Orwellian. He was referring to the science-fiction classic *1984*, written by British author George Orwell and published in 1949. The novel depicts Oceania, a futuristic totalitarian state led by a dictator called Big Brother. Big Brother's Thought Police carries out unchecked electronic spying into the private lives of Oceania's citizens, including that of the book's main character, Winston Smith. The following passage describes this surveillance:

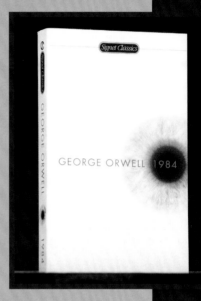

The telescreen received and transmitted simultaneously. Any sound that Winston made, above the level of a very low whisper, would be picked up by it, moreover, so long as he remained within the field of vision which the metal plaque commanded, he could be seen as well as heard. There was of course no way of knowing whether you were being watched at any given moment. How often, or on what system, the Thought Police plugged in on any individual wire was guesswork. It was even conceivable that they watched everybody all the time. But at any rate they could plug in your wire whenever they wanted to. You had to live—did live, from habit that became instinct—in the assumption that every sound you made was overheard, and, except in darkness, every movement scrutinized.

Winston kept his back turned to the telescreen. It was safer; though, as he well knew, even a back can be revealing.

Leon ordered the government to stop collecting data but then stayed, or stopped, his own order, "in light of the significant national security interests at stake," he explained. The stay allowed the NSA spying programs to continue. The US Department of Justice appealed Leon's ruling, and the case remains unresolved.

A few months later, in the spring of 2014, the US House of Representatives passed the USA Freedom Act, a bill that would limit the bulk collection of US phone data. The act was introduced to the Senate in July 2014, where it was voted down in November. Congress is expected to take up the issue again in June 2015, when a law called the Patriot Act expires. That law, passed after the 9/11 attacks, provided a legal basis for the bulk phone data collection.

In August 2013, a group called Restore the Fourth led a protest in New York City against NSA spying. The group's name refers to the Fourth Amendment, which protects US citizens from unreasonable government searches.

CHAPTER 5

THE PEOPLE PUSH BACK

As twenty-first century technologies have made it increasingly difficult to ensure individual privacy, many people are pushing back. For example, in 2013 British computer scientist Tim Berners-Lee, who in 1989 devised the network that would come to be called the World Wide Web, launched a campaign called the Web We Want. "Now is the time for citizens to mobilise to demand that governments and companies respect and protect our basic freedoms online." Berners-Lee stated. He called for a "national bill of rights for the internet—so that we can all build the web we want, and freely use its power to create the world we want." This bill of rights would include "freedom of expression online and offline," the "protection of personal user information and the right to communicate in private."

Others have weighed in as well. Maciej Cegłowski, a former engineer at Yahoo, remarked that the Internet "is getting . . .creepy. Everything is tracked forever, not just by sneaky governments, but by advertisers who see any human relationship as a sales opportunity." He advocates regulation of data collection and strict rules on how long data can be stored—"maybe three months, six months, three years. I don't really care, as long as it's not fifty years, or forever." American computer scientist Jaron Lanier, a leader in the world of virtual reality, objects to the prevailing Internet business model—in which companies make money by selling users' data. Lanier says that individuals should own their own data and that they, not commercial businesses, should be the ones to earn the profit. He wrote, "People ought to be paid for value they contribute that can be sent or stored on a digital network." *New York Times* business columnist Joe Nocera has called for tighter government regulation of social media sites and data brokers, stronger privacy settings on browsers, and more transparency—so that computer users know what data is being collected, when it is collected, and whom is collecting it.

Author Julia Angwin believes that the digital privacy movement is picking up speed. "It all reminds me of the early days of the organic food movement," she writes, "when buying organic often meant trekking to inconveniently located, odd-smelling stores and paying high rates for misshapen apples. Only the devoted few were willing to suffer the hassles. Over time, however, the number of people worried about chemicals in their food grew large enough to support a robust market. . . . A similar evolution in the personal-data-protection market is under way."

I'LL SEE YOU IN COURT

In the United States, rules concerning digital privacy are quickly changing as cases work their way through the legal system. For instance, in July 2013, the New Orleans-based Fifth Circuit Court of Appeals ruled that law enforcement does not need a search warrant to collect cell phone location data from phone companies. In other words, if the police want to know where you've been hanging out for the last six months, they can go to your phone company, which tracks your cell phone everywhere it goes (and presumably everywhere you go with it), and request those records—without first getting a search warrant.

The court's decision was based on a legal concept known as the third-party doctrine, which allows the government to access information that an individual has given voluntarily to a third party—in this case, the phone company. Privacy advocates decried the ruling, noting that the third-party doctrine was developed in the late 1970s, long before the era of cell phones. What's more, cell phones have become so intertwined with work, social life, banking, and other daily activities that many Americans couldn't function without them. Thus privacy advocates argue that it is a stretch to say that callers *voluntarily* give their location information to phone companies. After all, there is no surefire way to turn off the GPS tracking on your cell phone, so the only way to avoid being tracked is not to use a cell phone at all—which isn't a viable option for most people.

Other court rulings have served to protect digital privacy rather than weaken it. In one case, police pulled over a driver in San Diego, California, because his car registration had expired. Without a warrant, the officers searched his car and discovered loaded guns. They also searched his cell phone and found evidence that connected him to a shooting. He was convicted and sentenced to fifteen years to life in prison. In another case, police looked through the call log on the cell phone of a woman in Boston, Massachusetts, again without a warrant. Based on information found in the phone, the officers arrested the woman for gun and drug crimes. The police justified their actions by saying that cell phones are like wallets and purses, which police can search without a warrant.

What Can You Do?

While courts and regulatory agencies around the world sort through questions of protecting Internet privacy, ordinary Internet users can take some basic measures on their own. For instance, you can switch from Google to DuckDuckGo, a search engine that does not track users' activities. You can also download Ghostery or Blur, free browser ad-ons that let you monitor and control third-party data collection.

Experts also advise against using one company for multiple functions. For instance, if you use Google for searching, have a Google Gmail account, and use Chrome, Google's browser, you're making it even easier for Google to track you—since all the company's services share data with one another.

For even more privacy, some computer users encrypt their data streams with a free service called Tor. (Using this service may slow connection speed, however.) If you're willing to pay for privacy, companies such as WiTopia and Strong VPN will strip your Internet protocol address (an identification number assigned to each device) from your data. That means that the data can't be traceable to your computer.

For cell phone users, privacy options are changing all the time, depending on the phone and the operating system. No matter what devices you have, the key is to remain vigilant. Regularly check privacy settings on your phone and computer and clean out your search history. Keep an eye out for new apps and services that can protect your phone and computer from privacy intrusions.

Finally, be smart about what you share online and with whom. For instance, sharing nude photos has been shown to be unwise. Some people even put masking tape over the camera lenses on their computers, in the unlikely event that someone has used malicious software to take control of their machines.

Several judges disagreed. In the Boston case, a lower court judge ruled that the police had violated the woman's Fourth Amendment rights by not getting a warrant. "Today, many Americans store their most personal 'papers' and 'effects' in electronic format on a cellphone, carried on the person," Judge Norman Stahl wrote in his decision, quoting part of the Fourth Amendment. "Searching a person's cellphone is like searching his home desk, computer, bank vault and medicine cabinet all at once," wrote another judge, this time regarding a case in Texas.

The San Diego and Boston cases went all the way to the US Supreme Court, the highest court in the nation. In June 2014, the court issued a strong affirmation of privacy rights in the twenty-first century. Chief Justice John Roberts noted that cell phones are "a digital record of nearly every aspect of [people's] lives—from the mundane to the intimate." He continued, "The fact that technology now allows an individual to carry such information in his hand does not make the information any less worthy of the protection for which the Founders fought." Roberts also noted that mobile devices are more than just phones. "They could just as easily be called cameras, video players, Rolodexes, calendars, tape recorders, libraries, diaries, albums, televisions, maps or newspapers," he wrote. He also declared that if a being from Mars were to visit Earth, it might conclude that cell phones were a critical part of the human body.

GOOGLE UNDER FIRE

Google has found itself on the receiving end of much criticism, as well as legal action, for what many say are violations of privacy rights. For instance, in 2010 Mario Costeja González, a lawyer from A Coruña, Spain, did a Google search on his own name and found links to unsettling newspaper articles. The articles, written in 1998, described the auction of his house, which he was forced to undertake to pay debts. Costeja González called himself a fan of Google, but he thought the articles were damaging to his financial reputation and irrelevant, especially since the auction had occurred more than a decade before. "There is data [on the Internet] that is not relevant and that affects your dignity and your private life," he complained.

Costeja González asked Google to take the links down, but the company refused. The articles had been published in a public newspaper, Google said, and it was simply making this information readily available to its users.

"Thanks to the efficiency of search engines, time no longer heals all wounds."

—*Christopher Caldwell,* Financial Times, *2014*

Costeja González took Google to court in the European Union, of which Spain is a member. After four years, the case arrived at the Court of Justice of the European Union, the EU's highest court, based in Luxembourg. In a stunning setback to Google, the court ruled that individuals have a "right to be forgotten"—a legal concept applying to "irrelevant," "outdated," or "otherwise objectionable" information. Google would have to remove the links (though the stories could still be found on the original news website). Moreover, Google would have to institute a process to review requests from any European user who wanted to have something removed from search results.

Spaniard Mario Costeja González fought for the right to be forgotten—that is, to have outdated and damaging information about him removed from Google search results. He won his case in a European court, but Americans do not have a similar right to be forgotten on Google searches.

Michael Fertik, chief executive of Reputation.com (a website that helps individuals suppress negative online material about themselves), applauded the decision. "For the first time, human dignity will get the same treatment online as copyright," he said. He explained that copyright holders have long had the ability to keep material off the Internet: "If Sony or Disney wants fifty thousand videos removed from YouTube, Google removes them with no questions asked. If your daughter is caught kissing someone on a cell-phone video, you have no option of getting it down. That's wrong." Columnist Christopher Caldwell of the UK *Financial Times* agreed. "Thanks to the efficiency of search engines, time no longer heals all wounds. It is reasonable to make Google exercise some of the responsibility for protecting people from being stalked by their own data."

But others argued that the decision could suppress free speech and also be used to hide the truth. For instance, a politician could request that Google remove an embarrassing story about him or her from search results—thus keeping important information from voters. "Lawmakers should not create a right so powerful that it could limit press freedoms or allow individuals to demand that lawful information in a news archive be hidden," wrote the *New York Times* editorial board. Critics say that the law essentially allows for the censorship of accurate public information. What's more, it leaves the decision about what is "irrelevant, "outdated," or "otherwise objectionable" in Google's hands. The company has assembled a team of lawyers to review the tens of thousands of requests to remove links that it has received since the European court made its decision. In about half of the cases, such as those involving politicians and other public figures, Google has decided not to remove the links, reasoning that information on public figures should be freely available. But "there are hard calls," admits David Price, one of the Google lawyers.

Although the EU decision affects only computer users in Europe, privacy experts say that it might inspire similar lawsuits in the United States. Because of the case, Facebook and other tech companies are carefully watching legal developments regarding user privacy.

CANDID CAMERA

Most computer users have taken at least one online virtual tour of a street, a neighborhood, or a city using a program called Google Earth, created with photos taken from satellites. Google's Street View is similar, but the photos are taken with ordinary cameras mounted on the roofs of cars. To create

Street View, which debuted in 2007, Google staffers drove up and down the city streets of more than fifty countries, along more than 5 million miles (8 million kilometers) of roadway, photographing the surrounding landscape and buildings to create a virtual map. With Street View, users can virtually tour a city or a neighborhood simply by moving a mouse or swiping their fingers. And because Street View cameras are mounted on top of cars, they are often able to take photos over hedges and fences, capturing pictures of residents in areas that were designed for privacy.

Google has received numerous complaints about Street View. Both the US Department of Homeland Security and the Department of Defense have banned Google from photographing military bases and other government facilities. The departments worry that potential terrorists could use the images to virtually case a building and locate its vulnerabilities. Around the world, concerned about citizens' privacy, many governments have put restrictions on Street View photography or blocked the project altogether.

To protect the privacy of individuals in Street View photos, Google blurs faces and license plate numbers. Those who feel like the blurring doesn't adequately hide their identities can request that Google blur the images even further. But even with blurring, it is sometimes possible to identify people in photos.

Global controversy over Street View flared in 2010 when German technology official Johannes Caspar discovered that Street View was also identifying wireless routers in private homes in Germany and in other nations. If a router was not password protected, Street View equipment would record any data on the network. In a fraction of a second, a Street View car could collect texts, e-mails, and photos as it drove past a home.

Eye in the Sky

In February 2014, a company in San Francisco, California, called Planet Labs launched twenty-eight satellites, each the size of a shoe box, from the International Space Station. The satellites, called doves, take pictures of Earth in real time, and Planet Labs sells the images to governments and businesses. Such pictures can be valuable to environmentalists tracking illegal logging activity, for example, or to insurance companies calculating storm damage. And unlike Google Earth or Google Street View photos of specific places, which might be taken only once every few years, Planet Labs photos are updated regularly. Robbie Schingler, cofounder of Planet Labs, says, "Our monitoring capability is always on. We are always taking a picture."

Also in 2014, both Google and Facebook purchased companies that build unmanned aircraft called drones, which can also be equipped with cameras for capturing real-time images. The US military already uses drones to take surveillance photos, shoot missiles, and drop bombs. Google will likely use its drones for advanced digital mapping. Facebook's drones will be similar to aerial Wi-Fi hot spots, providing Internet access in more places around the world.

But such technology raises further concerns about assaults on privacy. As *New York Times* columnist Maureen Dowd asked, "Can we really trust Google . . . whose Street View vehicles secretly scooped up data around the world, with drones?"

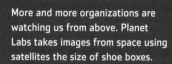

More and more organizations are watching us from above. Planet Labs takes images from space using satellites the size of shoe boxes.

Street View cameras have taken millions of images of locations around the world. The Street View program has been criticized, not only for photographing private spaces but also because its camera cars have secretly collected data from wireless networks.

"It was one of the biggest violations of data protection laws that we had ever seen," Caspar said. "We were very angry." When news of the data collection broke, Reinhold Harwart, mayor of a small German town, organized a protest. "The main feeling was: Who gives Google the right to do this?" said Harwart. "We were outraged that Google would come in, invade our privacy and send the data back to America, where we had no idea what it would be used for."

After these revelations, authorities in more than a dozen countries, including the United States, investigated Street View. Google defended itself, saying at first that the data collection had been accidental and that it had gathered only technical data about wireless networks, not about content traveling over those networks. The Federal Communications Commission (FCC), which regulates radio, TV, satellite, and other electronic communications in the United States, rejected this argument. It ruled that Google had acted deliberately to collect the data. The FCC also fined Google $25,000 for obstructing its investigation, saying that Google had not been forthcoming with information and had otherwise failed to cooperate with investigators. A group of thirty-seven US states also brought a lawsuit against Google for invading citizens' privacy through Street View data collection. In 2013 Google paid $7 million to settle that suit.

This Nest thermostat links to residents' smartphones. The ever-expanding network of digitally connected devices is called the Internet of Things.

CHAPTER 6

THE INTERNET OF THINGS

In the first decade of the 2000s, former Apple engineer Tony Fadell took time off to build a vacation home. In the process, he observed that many home appliances incorporated little or no Internet technology. They didn't seem to do much beyond their assigned tasks of heating or cooling food, washing clothes, and checking for smoke and fire. Fadell also thought the appliances were bland and unattractive. These ideas inspired him to found a company called Nest, to create home appliances that connected to the Internet.

Nest's first product was a thermostat. To replace the commonly used programmable box that turns home heating and air-conditioning systems on and off and makes a room warmer or cooler, Nest created an interactive "smart thermostat." The smart thermostat connects with residents' smartphones to record their home heating preferences. The thermostat then adapts, lowering temperatures in the house when residents are not home, for instance. This system can result in lower energy use and lower energy bills.

For the Nest thermostat to operate effectively, it must have access to users' real-time locations. In effect, the thermostat tracks a home's residents. And the more information the thermostat gathers about residents, such as their daily schedules, locations within the home, and temperature preferences, the more effective it will be. Nest has also created Nest Protect, which also syncs with residents' smartphones, alerting them to smoke, fire, or unsafe levels of carbon monoxide in their homes. In 2014 Google bought Nest for $3.2 billion.

Nest and other companies have created additional smart appliances; commentators have labeled this network of digitally connected devices the Internet of Things. With the Internet of Things, your refrigerator can monitor what's in it and remind you via smartphone that you're out of eggs. Your toothbrush can monitor how effectively you're brushing your teeth. Your athletic shoes can track the miles you've run and send the data to your smartphone.

Key components of the Internet of Things are electronic sensors that recognize and respond to physical stimuli, such as heat, pressure, light, sound, and motion. Many businesses and industries use sensors and the Internet of Things. For instance,

Online One-Liners

The fact that Google has purchased Nest sets off alarm bells among those who worry about Google's massive amount of data collection. Technology writer James Gleick, who bought a Nest thermostat for his home, jokes, "Now Google not only knows what books I'm reading, but they also know whether I'm shivering while I'm reading them." Another tech writer tweeted, "If your house is burning down, you'll now get gmail ads for fire extinguishers."

sensors in warehouses keep track of inventory and send data to company computers. Sensors in buildings monitor electricity use and send that data to computers as well. Managers can analyze this data to determine how to run machinery more efficiently, safely, and cheaply.

Modern cars are equipped with a variety of sensors that monitor speed, GPS location, gas mileage, tire pressure, and much more. This data is stored in a computer inside the car. Previously, only mechanics could access this data, when cars came into a shop for repair. But modern smartphone apps allow drivers to connect their phones with their car computers, providing advance warning of mechanical problems. Such warnings can keep drivers safer, alerting them when a part needs to be replaced for continued safe driving, for instance. The warnings can also save drivers money by prompting them to take care of minor car maintenance that can prevent major and expensive repairs. Experts say that by 2020, more than fifty billion sensors will be connected to the Internet of Things.

THE INTERNET ON YOU

The Internet of Things has also come to clothing and personal accessories. "A new device revolution is at hand," writes Bill Wasik, senior editor at *Wired* magazine. "Just as mobile phones and tablets displaced the once dominant PC, so wearable devices are poised to push smartphones aside."

The Internet has come to watches, eyeglasses, clothing, and athletic gear. At the 2014 US Open tennis tournament, for example, the ball boys wore shirts equipped with sensors that collected data on their heart and breathing rates. The Apple Watch, introduced in summer 2014, offers many iPhone features, including messaging, telephoning, and a range of apps, right on

Google Glass is an example of wearable technology. The device places an Internet display in front of the user's eyes. It can also be used like a smartphone to take photos and videos, record sound, send text messages, and make phone calls.

the wearer's wrist. The watch's activity app graphs data such as calories burned and how long the wearer has been standing up. The wearer can sync up this data with other health and fitness apps on the watch.

With Google Glass, Google has led the way with wearable tech. The device offers the viewer instant access to the Internet, with pages projected onto a display in front of the wearer's eye. Award-winning American novelist Gary Shteyngart wrote about his experience using Google Glass on a typical day in New York. In this 2013 *New Yorker* article, he is "the man":

> The man jerks his head, and slides his finger against the
> right temple of the glasses, across the so-called touch pad.

A pink rectangle above his field of vision, which looks like a twenty-five-inch television screen floating some eight feet away from him, is replaced by another message: ". . . flight 150 225pm delayed." . . . Another flick of the index finger, and a different screen clicks into place. Now it would appear that someone named Chris Brown is defending himself on Twitter and that a water bed for cows has been developed. . . . The man feels a tingle at the back of his ear, and a voice tells him his friend Christine Lee is ready to do a video call, also called a "hangout." The image of Christine at her desk beams above the man's right eye. He can see her and she, in turn, can see everything he sees through his glasses, the quiet green streetscape of East Eighty-eighth Street [in New York] streaming on her computer screen. He's going to go to the Guggenheim [Museum] later and promises her that she will be able to watch the new James Turrell [art] exhibition through his eyes.

Google Glass has generated a backlash. Privacy advocates note that the device can be used to take secret photos and videos and to record private conversations. Were you to try to do such things using a cell phone, you'd have to hold the phone noticeably. But with Google Glass, you can start recording with just a tap of a finger or a quiet command word, without anyone knowing or hearing. Many types of businesses prohibit customers from wearing Google Glasses on their premises. These businesses include banks, which worry about Google Glass wearers sneaking up behind other customers and taking pictures of account numbers; movie theaters, which don't want Google Glass wearers to secretly record entire movies, which can then be posted online; and hospitals, for concern about patient privacy. Some state governments have banned driving in Google Glasses, which can distract drivers, possibly leading to traffic accidents. In January 2015, Google announced that it was redesigning Glass, to make it more visually appealing to wearers and to upgrade its technology. Although Google has not announced a launch date for the redesigned Glass, tech visionaries believe that by the 2020s, the technology will be common in eyeglasses, sunglasses, and contact lenses.

THE INTERNET INSIDE YOU

Experts say that the Internet of Things will not only allow external web access but will soon offer web access from *within* you. Imagine sensors in your body, monitoring your health in real time, all of it instantaneously shared on a social media network. Health monitoring devices such as Fitbit track every step the user takes, including distance traveled and elevation gained (for those climbing mountains, for instance). At night, it monitors sleep patterns. By tracking this information, Fitbit can calculate how many calories the user is burning and other health measures. Another new device monitors babies' breathing rates, skin temperature, and sleeping position and sends the data to parents. A company called Proteus, named after a shrunken submarine that travels through the human body in the 1966 film *Fantastic Voyage*, has created a medicinal pill containing a sensor. When a patient swallows the pill, the sensor sends a signal to a patch on the patient's skin, which in turn alerts a doctor or a caregiver via smartphone that the patient has taken his or her medicine. The technology, which is already being sold in the United Kingdom, is designed for elderly people who might forget to take needed medications.

"It detects your posture, so you know when you need to reposition yourself. [It measures] blood and tissue oxygen, your red blood cell count, and things like step count. As you know, doctors recommend about 10,000 steps a day, and this will show you how close you're getting."

—Dave Eggers, The Circle, *futuristic novel, description of a medical sensor in someone's body, 2013*

Such technology has enormous potential to improve health and save lives. The amount of data the technology gathers, however, can be extraordinary and very intimate. Some people worry that the technology might be abused. For instance, what if a business knew more about your health than you did and used this information to deny you a job or health insurance or to try to sell you pharmaceutical products? These questions are unresolved and will undoubtedly surface as technology develops.

WHICH FUTURE DO WE WANT?

The rapid concentration of power and data into the hands of governments and tech companies could end privacy as we have historically understood it. Imagine this future scenario: We live in a world in which every square foot is under some kind of camera surveillance. The images taken by these cameras are scanned with facial recognition software to identify the people in the pictures, as well as their locations and activities. That data is combined with data from each individual's computers, smartphones, and other devices. Each person's data is aggregated, analyzed, and compared to billions of other data points generated by and collected from other individuals. Computer systems crunch all this data to learn each person's habits, thoughts, needs, and desires. Over time, this system grows more and more sophisticated and ultimately knows what individuals want before they know it themselves. At the same time, the information is also sold to the highest bidder, who uses it to sell products or to deny citizens opportunities, to influence their opinions, or to ensure that those in power remain in power. In fact, this scenario is not at all far-fetched. The world we live in is only steps away from operating this way.

The stakes are enormous. Privacy is about far more than just being left alone. It is about the space in which individuals can be free and can be themselves. This privacy is at the heart of a free democratic society, and many experts caution that if we lose our privacy, we lose our freedom.

Glenn Greenwald, the journalist who helped publicize Edward Snowden's revelations about NSA spying, summarizes the potential and the hazards of a wired society in the introduction to his book *No Place to Hide: Edward Snowden, the NSA, and the U.S. Surveillance State*. He writes, "Converting the Internet into a system of surveillance . . . turns [it] into a tool of repression, threatening to produce the most extreme and oppressive weapon of state intrusion human history has ever seen."

Greenwald concludes his introduction by stating that humankind stands at a crossroads. He asks, "Will the digital age usher in the individual liberation and political freedoms that the Internet is uniquely capable of unleashing? Or will it bring about a system of omnipresent monitoring and control, beyond the dreams of even the greatest tyrants of the past? Right now, either path is possible. Our actions will determine where we end up."

Source Notes

5 Eric Schmidt and Jared Cohen, *The New Digital Age: Reshaping the Future of People, Nations and Businesses* (New York: Knopf, 2013), 36.

5 Ibid.

6 Glenn Greenwald, "What I've Learned," *Esquire*, January 2014, http://www.esquire.com/news-politics/news/a26255/glenn-greenwald-interview-0114/

6 Mikko Hyppönen, "Why Should You Be Worried about NSA Surveillance?," *NPR*, January 31, 2014, http://www.npr.org/programs/ted-radio-hour/265352348/the-end-of-privacy.

6 Kate Murphy, "How to Muddy Your Tracks on the Internet," *New York Times*, May 2, 2012, http://www.nytimes.com/2012/05/03/technology/personaltech/how-to-muddy-your-tracks-on-the-internet.html.

8 "Fourth Amendment," Cornell University Law School, accessed February 25, 2015, http://www.law.cornell.edu/constitution/fourth_amendment.

10 Peggy Noonan, "What We Lose If We Give Up Privacy, *Wall Street Journal*, August 16, 2013, http://online.wsj.com/articles/SB10001424127887323639704579015101857760922.

10 Maureen Dowd, "Game of Drones," *New York Times*, April 15, 2014, http://www.nytimes.com/2014/04/16/opinion/game-of-drones.html.

12 Monika Bauerlein and Clara Jeffery, "Where Does Facebook Stop and the NSA Begin?," *Mother Jones*, November/December 2013, 24.

12 Joel Stein, "Data Mining: How Companies Now Know Everything about You," *Time*, March 10, 2011, http://content.time.com/time/magazine/article/0,9171,2058205,00.html.

14 Julia Angwin, *Dragnet Nation: A Quest for Privacy, Security, and Freedom in a World of Relentless Surveillance* (New York: Times, 2014), 32.

14–15 Stein, "Data Mining."

15 Julia Angwin, "The Web's New Gold Mine: Your Secrets," *Wall Street Journal*, July 30, 2010, http://online.wsj.com/articles/SB10001424052748703940904575395073512989404.

16   Fred Vogelstein, "And Then Steve Said, 'Let There Be an iPhone,'" *New York Times*, October 4, 2013.

16–17 Amir Efrati, Scott Thurm, and Dionne Searcey, "Mobile-App Makers Face U.S. Privacy Investigation," *Wall Street Journal*, April 5, 2011, http://online.wsj.com/articles/SB1000142405274 87038063045762429238804770968.

17   Jennifer Valentino-Devries, "What Can You Do? Not Much," *Wall Street Journal*, December 18, 2010, http://online.wsj.com /articles/SB10001424052748703929404576022140902538 236.

17   Aaron Pressman, "Big Data Could Create an Era of Big Discrimination," *Yahoo*, October 14, 2013, http://finance .yahoo.com/blogs/the-exchange/big-data-could-create-era-big -discrimination-191444085.html.

18   "First Amendment," Cornell University Law School, accessed February 25, 2015, http://www.law.cornell.edu/constitution /first_amendment.

18   "Fourth Amendment," Cornell University Law School.

18   Olivia Campbell, "Acxiom: The Data Collection Company You've Never Heard Of," *Online Privacy Blog*, March 17, 2014, http:// www.abine.com/blog/2014/acxiom-data-collection-company/.

18   Emily Steel, "Privacy Campaigners Attack Data Broker over 'Transparency' Move," *Financial Times*, September 5, 2013, http://www.ft.com/intl/cms/s/0/2220ac1a-15bb-11e3-950a -00144feabdc0.html#axzz3I1r2pvH7.

19   Ibid.

21–22 David Kirkpatrick, *The Facebook Effect* (New York: Simon & Schuster, 2010), 142.

22   "Scientific Marketing," Marketing-Schools.org, accessed February 25, 2015, http://www.marketing-schools.org/types -of-marketing/scientific-marketing.html.

22   Stein, "Data Mining."

22   Kate Kaye, "Will Transparency Help Big Data Face Down Its Critics," *Advertising Age*, September 9, 2013, http://adage.com /article/dataworks/transparency-big-data-face-critics/244037/.

23   Angwin, "Web's New Gold Mine."

23   Stein, "Data Mining."

25   Charles Duhigg, "How Companies Learn Your Secrets," *New York Times*, February 16, 2012, http://www.nytimes.com /2012/02/19/magazine/shopping-habits.html?pagewanted=all.

25   Ibid.

26   Ibid.

27   Ibid.

27   Ibid.

27   Lori Andrews, *I Know Who You Are and I Saw What You Did: Social Networks and the Death of Privacy* (New York: Free Press, 2012), 45.

28   James P. Steyer, *Talking Back to Facebook: The Common Sense Guide to Raising Kids in the Digital Age* (New York: Scribner, 2012), 50.

29   Ron Lieber, "American Express Kept a (Very) Watchful Eye on Charges, *New York Times*, January 30, 2009, http://www .nytimes.com/2009/01/31/your-money/credit-and-debit -cards/31money.html?pagewanted=all.

29   Lori Andrews, "Facebook Is Using You," *New York Times*, February 4, 2012. http://www.nytimes.com/2012/02/05/ opinion/sunday/facebook-is-using-you.html?pagewanted=all&_r=0.

29–30   Ibid.

30   Michael Schrage, "Big Data's Dangerous New Era of Discrimination," *Harvard Business Review*, January 29, 2014, http://blogs.hbr.org/2014/01/big-datas-dangerous-new-era-of -discrimination/.

31   Pressman, "Big Data."

33   Jan Hoffman, "A Girl's Nude Photo, and Altered Lives," *New York Times*, March 26, 2011, http://www.nytimes.com/2011/03/27 /us/27sexting.html?pagewanted=all.

33–34   Ibid.

34   Ibid.

34   "Jennifer Lawrence Calls Photo Hacking a 'Sex Crime,'" *Vanity Fair*, October 8, 2014, http://www.vanityfair.com/vf-hollywood /2014/10/jennifer-lawrence-cover.

34   Alex Hern and Dominic Rushe, "Google Threatened with $100m Lawsuit over Nude Celebrity Photos," *Guardian* (London), October 2, 2014, http://www.theguardian.com/technology /2014/oct/02/google-lawsuit-nude-celebrity-photos.

36 Charlotte Collins, "Snapchat Leaks Approximately 98,000 Pictures, Videos," *Daily Illini,* accessed February 25, 2015, http://m.dailyillini.com/news/article_18789704-58a4-11e4-a1d6 -0017a43b2370.html?mode=jqm.

36 Sarah Perez, "Majority of Top Messaging Apps and Tools Fail EFF's Security Review," *Techcruch,* November 5, 2014, http:// techcrunch.com/2014/11/05/majority-of-top-messaging-apps -and-tools-fail-effs-security-review/.

37 Andrews, I Know Who You Are, 56.

38 David Segal, "Mugged by a Mug Shot Online," *New York Times,* October 5, 2013. http://www.nytimes.com/2013/10/06 /business/mugged-by-a-mug-shot-online.html?pagewanted=all.

39 "Facebook Faces Criticism on Privacy Change," *BBC News,* December 10, 2009, http://news.bbc.co.uk/2/hi/8405334.stm.

39 Jenna Wortham, "Your Life on Facebook, in Total Recall," *New York Times,* December 15, 2011.

41 Angwin, *Dragnet Nation,* 11.

42 Andrews, *I Know Who You Are,* 111.

43 Ibid., 113.

43 Ibid., 112.

46–47 Heather Kelly, "After Boston: The Pros and Cons of Surveillance Cameras," *CNN,* April 26, 2013, http://www.cnn .com/2013/04/26/tech/innovation/security-cameras-boston -bombings/.

47 "Biometric Technology Takes Off," editorial, *New York Times,* September 20, 2013, http://www.nytimes.com/2013/09/21/ opinion/biometric-technology-takes-off.html.

47 Hyppönen, "Why Should You Be Worried?"

48 Jay Stanley, "New Public Safety Broadband Network: Tool for a Domestic Secret Police?," *Free Future,* September 17, 2012, https://www.aclu.org/blog/technology-and-liberty-free-speech -national-security/new-public-safety-broadband-network-tool.

50 Craig Timberg and Ellen Nakashima, "FBI's Search for 'Mo,' Suspect in Bomb Threats, Highlights Use of Malware for Surveillance," *Washington Post,* December 6, 2013, http://www .washingtonpost.com/business/technology/2013/12/06 /352ba174-5397-11e3-9e2c-e1d01116fd98_story.html.

51   Laura Poitras, "The Program," *New York Times*, August 22, 2012, http://www.nytimes.com/2012/08/23/opinion/the -national-security-agencys-domestic-spying-program.html.

51   Peter Maass, "How Laura Poitras Helped Snowden Spill His Secrets," *New York Times*, August 13, 2013, http://www .nytimes.com/2013/08/18/magazine/laura-poitras-snowden .html?pagewanted=all.

51   Ibid.

54   Oliver Stone and Peter Kuznick, "Obama Is Laying the Foundations of a Dystopian Future," *Financial Times*, July 10, 2013, http://www.ft.com/intl/cms/s/0/de81a466-e40d-11e2 -91a3-00144feabdc0.html#axzz3ShS8zweg.

54   "Surveillance: A Threat to Democracy," editorial, *New York Times*, June 11, 2013, http://www.nytimes.com/2013 /06/12/opinion/surveillance-a-threat-to-democracy.html.

54   Josh Keating, "Rousseff's Cybernationalism," *Slate*, September 24, 2013, http://www.slate.com/blogs/the_world_/2013/09/24 /brazilian_president_dilma_rousseff_slams_u_s_surveillance_at_ the_united.html.

55   Ellen Nakashima and Joby Warrick, "For NSA Chief, Terrorist Threat Drives Passion to 'Collect It All,'" *Washington Post*, July 14, 2013, http://www.washingtonpost.com/world/national -security/for-nsa-chief-terrorist-threat-drives-passion-to-collect -it-all/2013/07/14/3d26ef80-ea49-11e2-a301-ea5a8116d211_ story.html.

55   Steven Levy, "How the U.S. Almost Killed the Internet," *Wired*, February 2014, 72.

55–56   Jonathan Weisman, "Boehner Calls Snowden a Traitor," *New York Times*, June 11, 2013, http://thecaucus.blogs.nytimes.com /2013/06/11/boehner-calls-snowden-a-traitor/.

56   "Transcript of President Obama's Jan. 17 Speech on NSA Reforms," *Washington Post*, January 17, 2014, http://www .washingtonpost.com/politics/full-text-of-president-obamas-jan -17-speech-on-nsa-reforms/2014/01/17/fa33590a-7f8c-11e3 -9556-4a4bf7bcbd84_story.html/.

56   Maass, "Laura Poitras."

57   "The 2014 Pulitzer Prize Winners, Public Service," Pulitzer.org, accessed February 25, 2015, http://www.pulitzer.org/citation /2014-Public-Service.

57 Ellen Nakashima and Ann E. Marimow, "Judge: NSA's Collecting of Phone Records Is Probably Unconstitutional," *Washington Post*, December 16, 2013, http://www.washingtonpost.com /national/judge-nsas-collecting-of-phone-records-is-likely -unconstitutional/2013/12/16/6e098eda-6688-11e3-a0b9 -249bbb34602c_story.html.

58 George Orwell, *1984* (1949; repr. New York: Knopf, 1992), 4–5.

59 Charlie Savage, "Judge Questions Legality of N.S.A. Phone Records," *New York Times*, December 16, 2013, http://www .nytimes.com/2013/12/17/us/politics/federal-judge-rules -against-nsa-phone-data-program.html.

60 Robert Cookson, "Berners-Lee Calls for 'Ordinary People' to Protect Web," *Financial Times*, December 5, 2013, http://blogs .ft.com/tech-blog/2013/12/tim-berners-lee-launches-campaign -for-ordinary-people-to-protect-the-web/.

60 "Webfuture: How Should the Web Change for the Future?," Web We Want, accessed February 25, 2015, https:// webwewant.org/about_us.

60–61 Maciej Ceglowski, "The Internet with a Human Face," Vimeo, posted by "beyond tellerrand," May 20, 2014, http://vimeo.com /102717446.

61 Jaron Lanier, *Who Owns the Future?* (New York: Simon & Schuster, 2013), 245.

61 Julia Angwin, "Has Privacy Become a Luxury Good?," *New York Times*, March 3, 2014, http://www.nytimes.com/2014/03/04 /opinion/has-privacy-become-a-luxury-good.html.

64 Adam Liptak, "Supreme Court Will Consider Whether Police Need Warrants to Search Cellphones," *New York Times*, January 17, 2014, http://www.nytimes.com/2014/01/18/us /supreme-court-to-consider-limits-of-cellphone-searches.html.

64 Adam Liptak, "Supreme Court Taking Up Police Searches of Data Troves Known as Cellphones," *New York Times*, April 27, 2014.

64 John Cassidy, "The Supreme Court Gets It Right on Cell-Phone Privacy, *New Yorker*, June 25, 2014, http://www.newyorker.com /news/john-cassidy/the-supreme-court-gets-it-right-on-cell -phone-privacy.

64   Robert Barnes, "Supreme Court Says Police Must Get Warrants for Most Cellphone Searches," *Washington Post*, June 25, 2014, http://www.washingtonpost.com/national/supreme-court-police-must-get-warrants-for-most-cellphone-searches/2014/06/25/e2ff1326-fc6b-11e3-8176-f2c941cf35f1_story.html.

64   Ibid.

65   Tobias Buck, "Google Admirer Delivers Bitter Defeat on Principle of Privacy," *Financial Times*, May 14, 2014, http://www.ft.com/intl/cms/s/0/fca8f7f8-db53-11e3-94ad-00144feabdc0.html#axzz3lIRQAz3J.

65   Christopher Caldwell, "Google Has to Be Censored—Free Speech Can Scar," *Financial Times*, May 16, 2014, http://www.ft.com/intl/cms/s/0/eccff7f6-dc3d-11e3-8511-00144feabdc0.html#axzz3M5A1s1F6.

65   Jeffrey Toobin, "The Solace of Oblivion," *New Yorker*, September 29, 2014, http://www.newyorker.com/magazine/2014/09/29/solace-oblivion.

66   David Streitfeld, "European Court Lets Users Erase Records on Web," *New York Times*, May 13, 2014, http://www.nytimes.com/2014/05/14/technology/google-should-erase-web-links-to-some-personal-data-europes-highest-court-says.html.

66   Toobin, "The Solace of Oblivion."

66   Caldwell, "Google Has to Be Censored—Free Speech Can Scar."

67   "Ordering Google to Forget," editorial, *New York Times*, May 13, 2014, http://www.nytimes.com/2014/05/14/opinion/ordering-google-to-forget.html.

67   Toobin, "Solace of Oblivion."

69   "Largest Flock of Earth-Imaging Satellites Launch into Orbit from Space Station," NASA, February 11, 2014, http://www.nasa.gov/mission_pages/station/research/news/flock_1/#.U0lHr14Q5Zg.

69   Dowd, "Game of Drones."

70   David Streitfeld and Kevin J. O'Brien, "Google Privacy Inquiries Get Little Cooperation," *New York Times*, May 22, 2012, http://www.nytimes.com/2012/05/23/technology/google-privacy-inquiries-get-little-cooperation.html?pagewanted=all.

70   Ibid.

73   Marcus Wohlsen, "What Google Really Gets Out of Buying Nest for $3.2 Billion," *Wired,* January 14, 2014, http://www.wired.com/2014/01/googles-3-billion-nest-buy-finally-make-internet-things-r.

74   Bill Wasik, "Try It On," *Wired,* January 2014, 92.

75–76   Gary Shteyngart, "O.K., Glass: Confessions of a Google Glass Explorer," *New Yorker,* August 5, 2013, http://www.newyorker.com/magazine/2013/08/05/o-k-glass.

78   Dave Eggers, *The Circle* (New York: Knopf, 2013), 154–155.

79   Glenn Greenwald, *No Place to Hide: Edward Snowden, the NSA, and the U.S. Surveillance State* (New York: Metropolitan, 2014), 6.

79   Ibid.

Glossary

beacon: a tracking tool, placed by a website or a third party on a user's browser, that can monitor cursor movements on web pages and capture words typed into websites

censor: to examine and supervise communications in order to suppress or delete anything considered objectionable; self-censorship occurs when individuals suppress their own communication, typically for fear of retribution by government.

cookie: a small file sent from a website to a user's web browser. The cookie keeps track of the user's activities on the site. Some cookies track users' activities from site to site across the web.

copyright: the exclusive right to reproduce, publish, sell, or distribute creative work

data aggregator: a company that buys or collects digital data from public and private sources, analyzes it, packages it, and sells it to businesses, governments, and other organizations

data mining: analyzing large amounts of data to uncover patterns

encryption: the process of turning data into a code that only authorized parties can access through a password

facial recognition software: computer software that scans photos of faces and measures facial features, such as the distance between the eyes, the shape of a nose, or the length of a forehead. The software can also detect a person's gender, approximate age, skin color, and mood. It is used by law enforcement to identify people in surveillance photos or videos.

Fourth Amendment: a portion of the US Constitution that prohibits unreasonable searches by the government. The amendment states that police and other government agents cannot search citizens' homes or possessions without a good reason and without authorization by a judge or court.

hack: to gain access to a computer or other communications device illegally

Health Insurance Portability and Accessibility Act (HIPAA): a US law, passed in 1996, that guards the privacy of citizens' medical records. The law spells out to what extent health insurers, health-care providers, pharmacies, and other businesses can use or disclose medical information without a patient's permission.

International Mobile Subscriber Identity (IMSI) catcher: a machine that sends out signals like those used by cell phone towers, only

stronger. When cell phones receive the signals, they report their
identifying information and location to the machine. Many police
departments use IMSI catchers to track suspects.

Internet of Things: a network of industrial machines, home appliances,
vehicles, and other items that are connected to the Internet, with
the ability to send and receive data

Next Generation Identification system: an FBI database containing
more than fifty million photographs of Americans, including mug
shots, photos taken for employee background checks, and images
from security cameras. Police departments across the nation can
tap into the system, which also includes a database of fingerprints.

Patriot Act: a law passed in 2001 that gives US law enforcement and
intelligence agencies expanded tools for searching and surveilling
US citizens as part of the fight against terrorism

privacy: the right to control whether or not your personal information is
disclosed, to whom it is disclosed, and when it is disclosed

right to be forgotten: a legal concept, applicable in the European
Union, stating that irrelevant, outdated, or objectionable material
about an individual can be deleted from Internet search results

scientific marketing: marketing based on statistical analysis of data

search warrant: a document issued by a judge or a court that
authorizes law enforcement to search a person's possessions,
home, or vehicle for evidence of criminal activity

sensor: a device that monitors or measures a physical stimulus, such
as heat, light, sound, or pressure, and transmits the information it
gathers to another device, such as a computer

surveillance: close watch kept over people by a government, another
authority, or another individual

terms-of-use agreements: sometimes called terms-of-service
agreements; agreements posted on websites that spell out the
rules of site usage. Terms-of-use agreements frequently include
privacy policies.

third party: on the Internet, a group that contracts with a website
to collect or buy data about the site's users, often without the
knowledge or permission of visitors to the site

weblining: using digital data to determine someone's race, gender,
income, ethnic group, sexual orientation, or other characteristic
and then discriminating against the person because of that
characteristic

Selected Bibliography

Andrews, Lori. "Facebook Is Using You." *New York Times*, February 4, 2012. http://www.nytimes.com/2012/02/05/opinion/sunday /facebook-is-using-you.html?pagewanted=all&_r=0.

———. *I Know Who You Are and I Saw What You Did: Social Networks and the Death of Privacy*. New York: Free Press, 2012.

Angwin, Julia. *Dragnet Nation: A Quest for Privacy, Security, and Freedom in a World of Relentless Surveillance*. New York: Times, 2014.

———. "Has Privacy Become a Luxury Good?" *New York Times*, March 3, 2014. http://www.nytimes.com/2014/03/04/opinion/has-privacy -become-a-luxury-good.html.

———. "The Web's New Gold Mine: Your Secrets." *Wall Street Journal*, July 30, 2010. http://online.wsj.com/articles/SB1000142405274870 3940904575395073512989404.

Assange, Julian. *Cypherpunks: Freedom and the Future of the Internet*. New York: OR, 2012.

Bauerlein, Monika, and Clara Jeffery. "Where Does Facebook Stop and the NSA Begin?" *Mother Jones*, November/December 2013, 24.

Duhigg, Charles. "How Companies Learn Your Secrets." *New York Times*, February 16, 2012. http://www.nytimes.com/2012/02/19 /magazine/shopping-habits.html?pagewanted=all.

Eisenberg, Anne. "Microsatellites: What Big Eyes They Have." *New York Times*, August 10, 2013. http://www.nytimes.com/2013/08 /11/business/microsatellites-what-big-eyes-they-have .html?pagewanted=all.

———. "What I've Learned." *Esquire*, January 2014. http://www.esquire .com/blogs/news/glenn-greenwald-interview-0114.

Hyppönen, Mikko, "Why Should You Be Worried about NSA Surveillance?" *NPR*, January 31, 2014. http://www.npr.org/programs/ted-radio-hour /265352348/the-end-of-privacy.

Kelly, Heather. "After Boston: The Pros and Cons of Surveillance Cameras." *CNN*, April 26, 2013. http://www.cnn.com/2013 /04/26/tech/innovation/security-cameras-boston-bombings/.

Kirkpatrick, David. *The Facebook Effect*. New York: Simon & Schuster, 2010.

Lanier, Jaron. *Who Owns the Future?* New York: Simon & Schuster, 2013.

Maass, Peter. "How Laura Poitras Helped Snowden Spill His Secrets." *New York Times*, August 13, 2013. http://www.nytimes.com/2012 /08/23/opinion/the-national-security-agencys-domestic-spying -program.html.

Mayer-Schoenberger, Viktor, and Kenneth Cukier. *Big Data: A Revolution That Will Transform How We Live, Work, and Think*. New York: Houghton Mifflin Harcourt, 2013.

Morozov, Evgeny. *To Save Everything, Click Here*. New York: PublicAffairs, 2013.

Murphy, Kate. "How to Muddy Your Tracks on the Internet." *New York Times*, May 2, 2012. http://www.nytimes.com/2012/05/03 /technology/personaltech/how-to-muddy-your-tracks-on-the -internet.html.

Nissenbaum, Helen. *Privacy in Context: Technology, Policy, and the Integrity of Social Life*. Stanford, CA: Stanford University Press, 2010.

Noonan, Peggy. "What We Lose If We Give Up Privacy." *Wall Street Journal*, August 16, 2013. http://online.wsj.com/articles /SB10001424127887323639704579015101857760922

Pariser, Eli. *The Filter Bubble: What the Internet Is Hiding from You*. New York: Penguin, 2011.

Poitras, Laura. "The Program." *New York Times*, August 22, 2012. http:// www.nytimes.com/2012/08/23/opinion/the-national-security -agencys-domestic-spying-program.html.

Pressman, Aaron. "Big Data Could Create an Era of Big Discrimination." *Yahoo*, October 14, 2013. http://finance.yahoo.com/blogs/the -exchange/big-data-could-create-era-big-discrimination-191444085.html.

Schmidt, Eric, and Jared Cohen. *The New Digital Age: Reshaping the Future of People, Nations and Businesses*. New York: Knopf, 2013.

Schrage, Michael. "Big Data's Dangerous New Era of Discrimination." *Harvard Business Review*, January 29, 2014. http://blogs.hbr.org /2014/01/big-datas-dangerous-new-era-of-discrimination/.

Segal, David. "Mugged by a Mug Shot Online." *New York Times*, October 5, 2013. http://www.nytimes.com/2013/10/06/business /mugged-by-a-mug-shot-online.html?pagewanted=all.

Toobin, Jeffrey. "The Solace of Oblivion." *New Yorker*, September 29, 2014. http://www.newyorker.com/magazine/2014/09/29 /solace-oblivion.

Wu, Timothy. *The Master Switch: The Rise and Fall of Information Empires*. New York: Vintage, 2010.

Further Information

Books

Brown, Tracy. *Facebook Safety and Privacy*. New York: Rosen Central, 2014.

Bryan, Dale-Marie. *Smartphone Safety and Privacy*. New York: Rosen Central, 2014.

Doeden, Matt. *Whistle-Blowers: Exposing Crime and Corruption*. Minneapolis: Twenty-First Century, 2015.

Eggers, Dave. *The Circle*. New York: Knopf, 2013.

Espejo, Roman. *Policing the Internet*. Detroit, MI: Greenhaven, 2012.

Gitlin, Marty, and Margaret J. Goldstein. *Cyber Attack*. Minneapolis: Twenty-First Century, 2015.

Greenwald, Glenn. *No Place to Hide: Edward Snowden, the NSA, and the U.S. Surveillance State*. New York: Metropolitan, 2014.

Isaacson, Walter. *Steve Jobs*. New York: Simon & Schuster, 2011.

Kellmereit, Daniel, and Daniel Obodovski. *The Silent Intelligence: The Internet of Things*. San Francisco: DnD Ventures, 2013.

McPherson, Stephanie Sammartino. *Tim Berners-Lee: Inventor of the World Wide Web*. Minneapolis: Twenty-First Century, 2010.

Merino, Noel. *Privacy*. Farmington Hills, MI: Greenhaven Press, 2015.

Orwell, George. *1984*. 1949. Reprint, New York: Knopf, 1992.

Rudder, Christian. *Dataclysm: Who We Are (When We Think No One's Looking)*. New York: Crown, 2014.

Singer, P. W., and Allan Friedman. *Cybersecurity and Cyberwar: What Everyone Needs to Know*. New York: Oxford UP, 2014.

Solove, Daniel. *Nothing to Hide: The False Tradeoff between Privacy and Security*. New Haven, CT: Yale University Press, 2013.

———. *Understanding Privacy*. Cambridge, MA: Harvard University Press, 2008.

Websites

American Civil Liberties Union: Internet Privacy
https://www.aclu.org/technology-and-liberty/internet-privacy
This web page from the ACLU offers articles about the Fourth Amendment, Edward Snowden, and other online privacy topics.

Common Sense Media: Privacy and Internet Safety
https://www.commonsensemedia.org/privacy-and-internet-safety
This web page discusses the ways in which young people can
protect their privacy on the web.

Electronic Privacy Information Center
https://www.epic.org
This nonprofit organization offers extensive information on digital
privacy issues, including legal questions and court cases.

Privacy Rights Clearinghouse
https://www.privacyrights.org
This website provides information on consumers' privacy rights,
especially in the area of data tracking.

Films

Citizenfour. DVD. Berlin: Praxis Films, 2014.
Citizenfour is Laura Poitras's Academy Award–winning
documentary film of her in-person interactions with Edward
Snowden in a hotel room in Hong Kong, where he first revealed the
breadth of NSA electronic surveillance.

The United States of Secrets, Parts 1 and 2. DVD. Arlington, VA: PBS
Video, 2014.
This comprehensive series reports on the US government
surveillance of citizens in the years since the terrorist attacks
of 9/11.

Index

Photo Acknowledgments

The images in this book are used with the permission of: Natalie Faye Image Source/Newscom, p. 4; JEFF TOPPING/REUTERS/Newscom, p. 8; Alexander Porter Image Source/Newscom, p. 12; © Eldadcarin/Dreamstime.com, p. 16; AP Photo/DANNY JOHNSTON, p. 19; © Mareen Fischinger/CORBIS, p. 20; © Keri Wiginton/Tribune News Service/Getty Images, p. 27; © Duc Dao/Shutterstock.com, p. 32; © Featureflash/Dreamstime.com, p. 35; AP Photo/Ronald Zak, p. 40; © John Moore/Thinkstock, p. 42; © Bigapplestock/Dreamstime.com, p. 44; RICHARD B. LEVINE/Newscom, p. 46; Paul Venning Image Source/Newscom, p. 49; BRIAN SNYDER/REUTERS/Newscom, p. 56; © Todd Strand/Independent Picture Service, p. 58; © Richard Levine/Alamy, p. 60; © epa european pressphoto agency b.v./Alamy, p. 66; KARL MONDON/MCT/Landov, p. 69; © Byrion Smith/flickr.com (CC BY 2.0), p. 70; © David Paul Morris/Bloomberg/Getty Images, p. 72; © iStockphoto.com/ferrantraite, p. 75; Maksim Kabakou/Shutterstock.com, number backgrounds throughout.

Front cover: © Maksim Kabakou/Shutterstock.com

About the Author

Brendan January is an award-winning author of more than twenty nonfiction books for young readers. Among his young adult titles for TFCB are *The Iranian Revolution*—a JLG selection and a NCSS/CBC Notable Social Studies Trade Book for Young People—and *Genocide: Modern Crimes against Humanity*—also a NCSS/CBC Notable Social Studies Trade Book for Young People and featured on VOYA's Nonfiction Honor List. He attended Haverford College in Pennsylvania and the Columbia Graduate School of Journalism in New York. He was also a Fulbright scholar in Germany. He lives with his wife and two children in Maplewood, New Jersey.